Best Practices to Help At-Risk Learners

Franklin P. Schargel

EYE ON EDUCATION
6 DEPOT WAY WEST, SUITE 106
LARCHMONT, NY 10538
(914) 833–0551
(914) 833–0761 fax
www.eyeoneducation.com

Library of Congress Cataloging-in-Publication Data

Schargel, Franklin P.
Best practices to help at-risk learners / Franklin P. Schargel.
     p. cm.
   ISBN-13: 978-1-59667-017-4
1. Dropouts—United States—Prevention. 2. Problem students—Education—United States. 3. Motivation in education—United States. 4. School improvement programs—United States. I. Title.
LC143.S2195 2005
371.93—dc22

                                                          2005029221

10 9 8 7 6 5 4 3

Editorial and production services provided by
Richard H. Adin Freelance Editorial Services
52 Oakwood Blvd., Poughkeepsie, NY 12603-4112
(845-471-3566)

Also Available from EYE ON EDUCATION

Helping Students Graduate
Jay Smink and Franklin P. Schargel

Dropout Prevention Tools
Franklin P. Schargel

Strategies to Help Solve Our School Dropout Problem
Franklin P. Schargel and Jay Smink

At-Risk Students
Reaching and Teaching Them, Second Edition
Richard Sagor and Jonas Cox

The Handbook for
Developing Supportive Learning Environments
Teddy Holtz Frank

Classroom Motivation from A to Z:
How to Engage Your Students in Learning
Barbara R. Blackburn

Dealing with Difficult Parents
And With Parents in Difficult Situations
Todd Whitaker and Douglas J. Fiore

Achievement Now!
How to Assure No Child is Left Behind
Dr. Donald J. Fielder

Student Transitions from Middle to High School:
Improving Achievement and Creating a Safer Environment
J. Allen Queen

Promoting a Successful Transition to Middle School
Patrick Akos, J. Allen Queen, and Christopher Lineberry

101 Answers for New Teachers and Their Mentors:
Effective Teaching Tips for Daily Classroom Use
Annette L. Breaux

Handbook on Differentiated Instruction
for Middle and High Schools
Sheryn Spencer Northey

Dedication

To Sandy, David, Howard, and Pegi, and
to the dedicated educational professionals who work with
at-risk learners.

About the Author

Franklin P. Schargel
Educator, Staff Developer, Trainer, Consultant, Author

Franklin Schargel, a native of Brooklyn New York, now residing in Albuquerque NM, is a graduate of the University of the City of New York. Franklin holds a Masters Degree in Secondary Education from City University and a second Masters Degree from Pace University in School Administration and Supervision. His career spans thirty-three years of classroom teaching, counseling, and eight years of supervision and administration as a school administrator. Additionally, Franklin taught a course in Dowling College's MBA Program.

Franklin served on the Guidelines Development Committee for the Malcolm Baldrige National Quality Award in Education and was, for two years, an examiner for the Baldrige Award. He also served as a judge for the Secretary of the Air Force Quality Award and a judge for the USA Today/RIT Quality Cup. He is the immediate past chair of the American Society of Quality's Education Division. Mr. Schargel was recently honored by the National Dropout Prevention Center's Crystal Star Award for "demonstrating clear evidence of success in dropout recovery, intervention, and prevention."

As Senior Managing Associate of his training firm, School Success Network, Franklin has presented countless workshops for educational, community, and business groups throughout the United States, Europe, Canada, and Latin America. His workshops are for teachers, administrators, counselors, support personnel, students, parents, business leaders, policymakers, and anyone else interested in building world-class schools. They cover a wide variety of topics, including addressing the at-risk school populations and dropout prevention, educational leadership, empowerment of staff, interactive learning, organizational change, parental involvement, problem solving, Career and Technical Education.

He is the author of five well-received books and many articles published in the leading educational journals and business magazines. Mr. Schargel has a regular monthly Internet column at www.guidancechannel.com.

Franklin's success in dramatically enhancing the learning process in his inner-city school, expanding parental involvement, increasing postsecondary school attendance, and significantly lowering the students' dropout rate, has been well documented in 25 books, 55 newspaper and magazine articles, and five internationally released videos (including a Public Broadcasting Special.) The United States Department of Education, Fortune Magazine, Business Week, and the New York Times have recognized his work.

Acknowledgements

Children are the least-represented people in our society. Because they do not vote, they are not directly represented in Congress or in state or local politics. Although there are groups who speak in their interest, such as the Children's Defense Fund, they are not as influential or as powerful as the AARP or the AFL-CIO, which represent other segments of our population.

As I travel around the country, I am impressed by the creativity and generosity of educators. They share a desire to help children and those who are involved in helping children. Their willingness to share and to help other educators to succeed is to be commended. I dedicate this book to those educators who share a love of children and a desire to help them.

The creation of this book, more than most, depended on the expertise, knowledge, creativity, and generosity of others. The contributions of many individuals and organizations have made this book possible. Their beneficence and willingness to share their knowledge and practical experience about effective practices, programs, and interventions, as well as their desire to help others succeed, is a tribute to them. You will find their names, their schools or programs, and their contact information at the end of this book.

I must thank a number of individuals who graciously shared their expertise with me. I was able to compile this book because of the individuals named here and below. Thanks to Ella Bell, Alabama School Board Member; Jennifer Brady, the Guidance Channel; Erlinda S. Gonzalez, Taos, New Mexico Town Council; Jim Lawson, Panama City, Florida, School System; and Jim Lockhart III, U.S. Department of Education. In addition, I thank the personnel of the National Dropout Prevention Center at Clemson University: Dr. Jay Smink (executive director), Dr. Terry Cash, Dr. Sam Drew, Marty Duckenfeld, John Peters, Mary Reimer, Linda Shirley, Susie Turbeville, and Dr. Ted Wesley.

I sincerely thank Robert Sickles, my publisher, who has always supported and encouraged my efforts from the very beginning.

Introduction

This book serves as a companion to *Strategies to Help Solve Our School Dropout Problem* and *Helping Students Graduate: A Strategic Approach To Dropout Prevention*. Both of those books, coauthored with Dr. Jay Smink, executive director of the National Dropout Prevention Center at Clemson University, supplied the *what* to do regarding at-risk youth and dropout prevention. This book supplies the *how* to do it.

Educators have long asked for specific tools to address the growing at-risk student population in our schools. The material in this book provides best practices taken from successful schools, school districts, and a variety of state and local programs. The *Helping* and *Strategies* books provided the foundation for this book. Whereas those books addressed the macro picture, this book focuses on the micro picture.

This book is an effective resource for those who are interested in establishing schools or programs to deal with at-risk students, for those who are currently involved in schools or programs, and for those who would like to improve what they are currently doing.

I have collected information from the U.S. Department of Education, state departments of education, colleagues, people I have met while presenting at or attending workshops, schools and programs that have been identified as successful in recovering dropouts, and other practices that have prevented at-risk students from turning into dropouts.

Why Is There a Need for This Book?

Educators want and need a set of reliable, field-tested, research-based, data-driven practices that will enable them to take advantage of what others have learned and to avoid the pitfalls others have faced and conquered. The first *Dropout Prevention Tools* book filled a vital need.

How To Read This Book

Like you, this book is unique, so there is no right way or wrong way to read it. It is as user friendly as we could make it. You may want to start with the first page and read all the way through, or you might see something that intrigues you and start there. Feel free to make the book your own, because it is. Mark up the book: Highlight the "good parts."

If you are like me—and most other educators—you buy books and put them on the shelf, hoping to get around to reading them someday. This book is designed to be used. We have tried to make this book user friendly in the following ways:

Modules:

This book is divided into 15 modules, one for each of the strategies identified in the *Strategies* and *Helping* books. Each module contains tools, graphs, charts, and rubrics pertaining to that particular strategy.

Designation by strategy:

In the *Strategies* and *Helping* books, the strategies were separated from one another. Similarly, the activities in this manual are presented individually so that the reader can investigate the different types of activities that are available. In reality, however, activities are rarely conducted independently. Highly effective schools and programs combine a number of strategies to render maximum impact on the at-risk problem. For example, many strategies apply to more than one section of the book. At the right-hand side of each page, you will find a list of strategies that can be applied for that particular technique.

Designation for user:

Classroom teachers will find every tool in this book useful. Some of them have added value for administrators, counselors, and special educators. On the left-hand side of each page, you will find a list of job titles whom I feel would benefit from each particular tool.

Designation by grade level:

On the right-hand side of each page, you will see the activities have been divided into grade-level designations (preschool, elementary, middle, high school, and all grade levels). This allows educators to choose which tool applies best to them.

Indexes:

There are five indexes at the back of the book: Indexes by strategy, by grade level, and for special educators, counselors, and administrators. There is no separate index for classroom teachers because all tools apply to them.

Permission to recopy:

Many authors prevent you from using their material through the use of copyright. I believe that we need to share information. You have permission to reproduce the contents of this book for educational purposes.

Large print:

The book uses a larger font than is found in most books to facilitate easy reproducing and reading of the material.

Will the Exercises Work For You?

All of the tools have been field tested. We know these tools, rubrics, and techniques have worked and have produced positive results. However, each school has its own culture and is unique. The tool must be customized for your community. (Simply using them without adapting them to your school's culture will render their effectiveness suboptimal). No one knows better than you what will work in your locale. I suggest that you try the tool the way it appears, then ask the people who have been involved in the deployment of the tool how they would improve the tool or its deployment.

After you have tried the tool, ask yourself the following questions:

What worked in this tool?

What made it work?

What needs to be improved or modified?

How do we make those modifications?

What do we have to measure to know that we have made the right improvements?

This Is a Work in Progress

What you hold in your hands is a work in progress. It surely will need to be modified, expanded, and corrected. I would like to know what you did with the tools. What worked? What modifications did you make that helped the tools work better? Do you have any tools or techniques that have proved successful with at-risk students? If so, would you be willing to share them and have them included in the next volume of this book?

If you would like to join me in this effort to help our colleagues, America's children, their parents, and the business community in this crucial effort to end the growth of our at-risk, potential school-dropout population, please contact me at franklin@schargel.com.

To find out when I will be presenting a workshop in your area or to learn about the other work I am doing, see my Web site, www.schargel.com.

Franklin P. Schargel
Albuquerque, New Mexico

15 Strategies

Since 1986, the National Dropout Prevention Center at Clemson University has been conducting and analyzing research in order to reduce America's dropout rate. It has identified 15 effective strategies that have the most positive impact on the dropout rate. These strategies have been implemented successfully at all education levels and in environments throughout the nation.

School and Community Perspective

Systemic Renewal

This is a continuing process of evaluating goals and objectives related to school policies, practices, and organizational structures as they affect a diverse group of learners.

School–Community Collaboration

When all groups in a community provide collective support to the school, a strong infrastructure sustains a caring, supportive environment in which youth can thrive and achieve.

Safe Learning Environments

A comprehensive violence-prevention plan, including conflict resolution, must deal with potential violence as well as crisis management. A safe learning environment provides daily experiences, at all grade levels, that enhance positive social attitudes and effective interpersonal skills in all students.

Early Interventions

Family Engagement

Research consistently finds that family engagement has a direct, positive effect on children's achievement and is the most accurate predictor of a student's success in school.

Early Childhood Education

Birth-to-five interventions demonstrate that providing a child with additional enrichment can enhance brain development. The most effective way to reduce the number of children who ultimately will drop out is to provide the best possible classroom instruction from the beginning of the school experience through the primary grades.

Early Literacy Development

Early interventions to help low-achieving students improve their reading and writing skills establish the necessary foundation for effective learning in all other subjects.

Basic Core Strategies

Mentoring and Tutoring

Mentoring is a caring, supportive, one-on-one relationship between a mentor and a mentee that is based on trust. Tutoring, also a one-on-one activity, focuses on academics and is an effective practice for addressing specific needs, such as reading, writing, or math competencies.

Service Learning

Service learning connects meaningful community service experiences with academic learning. This teaching and learning method promotes personal and social growth, career development, and civic responsibility, and it can be a powerful vehicle for effective school reform at all grade levels.

Alternative Schooling

Alternative schooling provides potential dropouts with a variety of options that can lead to graduation. Programs pay special attention to the student's individual social needs and academic requirements for a high school diploma.

After-School Opportunities

Many schools provide after-school and summer enhancement programs that eliminate information loss and inspire interest in a variety of areas. Such experiences are especially important for students who are at risk of school failure because they fill the afternoon "gap time" with constructive and engaging activities.

Making the Most of Instruction

Professional Development

Teachers who work with youth at high risk of academic failure need to feel supported and need an avenue by which they can continue to develop skills and techniques and learn about innovative strategies.

Active Learning

Active learning embraces teaching and learning strategies that engage and involve students in the learning process. Students find new and creative ways to solve problems, achieve success, and become lifelong learners when educators show them there are different ways to learn.

Educational Technology

Technology offers some of the best opportunities for delivering instruction to engage students in authentic learning, addressing multiple intelligences, and adapting to students' learning styles.

Individualized Instruction

Each student has unique interests and past learning experiences. An individualized instructional program for each student allows for flexibility in teaching methods and motivational strategies that consider these individual differences.

Career and Technical Education

A quality career and technical education program and a related guidance program are essential for all students. School-to-work programs recognize that youth need specific skills to prepare them to measure up to the larger demands of today's workplace.

These strategies were developed for use in *Strategies to Help Solve Our School Dropout Problem* and *Helping Students Graduate: A Strategic Approach to Dropout Prevention* by Franklin Schargel and Jay Smink, published by Eye on Education, Inc.

Table of Contents

Family Engagement

Research consistently finds that family engagement has a direct, positive effect on children's achievement and is the most accurate predictor of a student's success in school. The following tools are included in this chapter:

How to Maximize the Effectiveness of Parent–Teacher Conferences, excerpted from *Working Together: Parent, Family and Community Involvement in Education Tool Kit,* New Mexico Department of Education and the Center for the Education and Study of Diverse Populations, September 2000. I am indebted to Jennifer Yahn of the New Mexico Department of Education for developing this material and making me aware of its existence.

Dealing with Unreceptive Parents, developed by Franklin P. Schargel.

How to Make Your School Family Friendly, developed by Franklin P. Schargel.

What Can Parents and Teachers Do If an Adolescent Begins to Fail in School? developed by ACCESS ERIC.

How To Maximize the Effectiveness of Parent–Teacher Conferences

Administrator   All Grade Levels   Family Engagement
Teacher   Professional Development
Special Educator

Parent–teacher meetings provide an excellent opportunity for home–school communication. Parents provide a valuable resource, important perspectives, and information that cannot be obtained elsewhere. Teachers need the help of parents to do the best possible job of educating every child and can help parents play an active role in education at home. Conferences are a time for listening and sharing. They also provide an opportunity for teachers to explain the curriculum and the criteria and grades used on report cards. Conferences are successful when teachers and the school district create a climate that invites collaboration with parents. Creating this climate requires planning and effort. The following suggestions are ways that teachers, principals, and the system can maximize the effectiveness of parent–teacher conferences.

Before the Conference

Principals and other district officials can coordinate activities and provide suggestions to teachers.

Prepare teachers for conferences:

- Use inservice meetings to orient teachers to the system's goals and effective procedures for conferences.
- Use role-playing exercises to help teachers, especially new teachers, to anticipate and deal positively with typical parent questions.
- Allot sufficient time for teachers to conduct conferences and provide substitutes if additional time is needed.
- Provide child care, refreshments, and transportation if needed.
- Arrange translation services and let parents know that they are available.
- Develop a flexible conference schedule that will provide options for parents who work or have more than one child in the school.
- Let parents know about upcoming conferences through a variety of channels—letters, newsletters, radio and television announcements, e-mail, PTA meetings, and community cable television channels.
- Survey parents to identify their areas of concern.
- Send parents a conference planning sheet that outlines a set of questions they may want to ask teachers.

- Ask parent volunteers to telephone other parents to encourage them to attend. Teachers have a role involving planning and preparation. The follow are some tips:
- Send a personal letter or card or make a phone call to remind parents about the meeting. Confirm the conference time.
- Indicate that individual conferences are being held with all parents and how important they are.
- Encourage parents to review classwork and tests that are brought home and to note questions, concerns, and comments to bring to the conference.
- Prepare for the conference by developing a conference folder or portfolio with samples of the student's work and a list of the teacher's concern and questions.
- Create a comfortable and private physical environment with enough adult-sized chairs and no desk separating the teacher from the parent.

During the Conference

- **Establish rapport with parents**—Develop a relationship with parents by asking them about their work, other children, or an interest you know they have.
- **Accept parents as advocates**—Provide parents with opportunities to speak about their children. Do not interpret a parent's advocacy as belligerence or criticism.
- **Emphasize the positive**—Indicate your appreciation of the unique qualities of the child.
- **Establish priorities**—Pick one or two areas for growth and improvement so that parents are not overwhelmed.
- **Involve parents in creating solutions to problems**—Ask parents what they can do to help their child's learning.
- **Action steps**—Close the conference with some action steps. Identify concrete suggestions for how the parents and teacher can help the child together. Provide resources and materials such as booklets that families can use at home to build student skills. Give parents specific times when they can call you, or provide parents with your school e-mail address.

After the Conference

Keep brief notes about the conference; follow through and remember to list the parent's concerns.

- Note and address suggestions made and questions raised during the conference.
- Keep parents informed of any steps that you or other school personnel have taken, and follow up with parents on actions that they were going to take.
- Share nonconfidential information about students and their families with colleagues such as counselors, social workers, and psychologists.
- Follow up the conference with a phone call or a note to all parents to your commitment to working as a team.

Dealing with Unreceptive Parents

Administrator
Counselor
Special Educator
Teacher

All Grade Levels

Family Engagement
Professional Development

Some parents of at-risk children do not know how to cope with their child's behavior. They may become hostile or aggressive during meetings. The following tool is designed to assist educators in dealing with argumentative parents.

- ◆ Bring documentation for what you are about to tell the parent.
  - Grades
  - Dates and times of phone calls
  - Copies of letters sent
- ◆ Listen to what the parent has to say.
- ◆ Keep calm and professional.
- ◆ Be prepared.
  - Questions
  - Positives
  - Compassion
- ◆ Open the lines of communication.
- ◆ Use prevention strategies. Call parents in advance and compliment their child when it is deserved.
- ◆ Know your limits. If you are unable to provide the assist parents in getting the help they need, refer them to someone who may be able to address the situation (such as a school social worker, guidance counselor, nurse, physiologist, or principal).
- ◆ End the conversation pleasantly. Thank the parents for coming. Tell them to keep in contact. Drop them a note thanking them for coming and suggest a continual dialogue. Document the conversation when you have a chance.

How To Make Your School Family Friendly

Administrator   All Grade Levels   Family Engagement
Special Educator   Professional Development
Teacher

- **Open the lines of communication.** Meet with representatives of the community, including church leaders and community-based organizations such as the chamber of commerce, Rotary, Lions, etc. Have them announce school events such as parent meetings, sporting events, and student performances. Give them tickets to sporting events and student performances.

- **Have student translators available for parents who speak a language other than English.**

- **Have staff make positive phone calls to parents.** Most phone calls made to homes tend to be negative. Parents who get positive phone calls appreciate it. Call parents and compliment the child for coming on time, being well prepared, or doing well on an examination or at a sporting or school event.

- **Have the school cleaned before parent meetings.** Parents notice.

- **Have student work hanging in classrooms.** Parents and students need a replicable model of what quality work looks like. Create a template by having student work hanging in classrooms and halls.

- **Have a "We Don't Want To Brag" bulletin board.** Put positive news on a bulletin board that parents will notice when they enter the school. The work may include positive news about faculty such as their participation in out-of school events or achievement of degrees. Newspaper articles about the success of students in contests, sports, or achievements should be included. Include information or letters from graduates who are in college, the workforce, or the military.

- **Hang graphs of student achievement.** Graphs showing improvements in testing and attendance can be placed in visible locations in the building. The graph lines should be going up, not down. Graphs should emphasize the positive, not the negative. For example, you want to show the number of students who graduate, not those who drop out.

- **Celebrate student success.** Find occasions to celebrate the success of students, whether it is in academics, sports, or student activities. Make sure to invite parents. Take instant pictures of parents celebrating with their children. The success should not create winners and losers. Ensure that every student can be a winner.

♦ **Hold a contest through your parent organization.** Prizes can be awarded to the parent who brings the most parents to a parent meeting, to the one who attends most frequently, or simply to a parent who shows up. Prizes may include free meals at a fast-food restaurant. (They are generally willing to give away meals.) No-cost prizes also may include tickets to school sporting events or performances.

♦ **Organize a family/faculty event.** Have parents and faculty sit down to "break bread" together. Have everyone bring something to eat (even if it is store-bought cookies.) The meeting might be held off site at a community center or church. This provides an opportunity for people to engage in conversation, which need not be about what takes place in school.

♦ **"Everyone, bring one."** Encourage parents who attend a meeting to bring the parents of one of their child's friends.

What Can Parents and Teachers Do
If an Adolescent Begins to Fail in School?

Administrator   Middle School   After-School Opportunities
Counselor   High School   Career and Technical Education
Special Educator   Family Engagement
Teacher   Professional Development
                                              School–Community Collaboration

ERIC identifies some characteristics of adolescents who are at risk of failing in school and offers advice on how parents and educators can assist them.

Common Characteristics of Adolescents
At Risk of School Failure

+ **Attention problems:** The student has a history of attention issues at school.
+ **Poor grades:** The student consistently performs at barely average or below-average levels.
+ **Retention:** The student has been retained in one or more grade levels.
+ **Absenteeism:** The student is absent five or more days per term.
+ **Lack of connection with school and community:** The student is not involved in sports, music, scouting, or extracurricular activities.
+ **Behavioral problems:** The student may be disciplined frequently in school or may show a sudden change in school behavior, such as withdrawing from classroom discussions.
+ **Lack of confidence:** The student believes that success is linked to natural intelligence rather than to hard work and that his or her own ability is insufficient and cannot be changed or improved.
+ **Limited goals for the future:** The student seems unaware of the career options that are available or how to attain those goals.

If an adolescent exhibits more than one of these characteristics, he or she will likely need assistance from parents and teachers to be successful in school.

How Can Parents and Teachers Respond?

When an adolescent is having difficulty, parents and teachers can assist by doing the following:

+ Making time to listen to the teenager's fears or concerns and trying to understand them.
+ Setting appropriate boundaries for behavior that are consistently enforced.

- Emphasizing the importance of study skills, hard work, and follow-through at home and school.
- Arranging tutoring or study group support for the teenager at the school or in the community through organizations such as the local YMCA or a local college or university.
- Providing a supportive home and school environment in which education is clearly valued.
- Encouraging the teenager to participate in one or more school activities.
- Becoming more involved in school activities by attending school functions, such as sporting events, concerts, science fairs, and plays, to show support for the school.
- Meeting as a team with the student and a school counselor to share expectations for the teenager's future and to figure out how the counselor can support his or her learning environment.
- Helping the teenager to think about career options by arranging visits to local companies and colleges, providing information about careers and vocational or college courses, and encouraging the teenager to participate in an internship or a career-oriented part-time job.

Encouraging the teenager to volunteer in the community or to participate in community groups, such as the YMCA, scouting, 4-H, religious organizations, or other service-oriented groups to provide an out-of-school support system.

Early Childhood Education

Birth-to-five interventions demonstrate that providing a child with additional enrichment can enhance brain development. The most effective way to reduce the number of children who ultimately will drop out is to provide the best possible classroom instruction from the beginning of the school experience through the primary grades. The following tools are included in this chapter:

What Are the Knowledge and Skills that Early Childhood Educators Need to Know in Serving the Needs of English-Language Learners? excerpted from *New Teachers for a New Century: The Future of Early Childhood Professional Preparation,* U.S. Department of Education, National Institute on Early Childhood Development and Education, February 2001.

How Parents and Teachers Can Aid Students in Learning about the Sounds of Spoken Language, adapted from *Teaching Our Youngest,* U.S. Department of Education and U.S. Department of Health and Human Services, Early Childhood Head Start Task Force, Washington, DC, 2002.

What Are the Knowledge and Skills that Early Childhood Educators Need to Know In Serving the Needs of English-Language Learners?

Administrator   Preschool   Early Childhood Education
Counselor   Elementary School   Family Engagement
Special Educator   Individualized Instruction
Teacher   Professional Development

With the increasing numbers of English-language learners, early childhood educators need to be aware and prepared to deal with this unique population. The U.S. Department of Education has developed a list of skills and knowledge for early childhood teacher preparation.

Language and Culture

◆ To understand theories of first and second language acquisition

◆ To validate students' culture

◆ To use communication styles that accommodate the language and culture of students and their families

◆ To demonstrate native-like proficiency in two or more languages and be able to communicate effectively in a variety of formal and informal sociocultural contexts

◆ To understand language, culture, family organization, patterns of authority, social organization, and knowledge forms and their influence on learning

◆ To provide focused stimulation for language development by modeling the target language and using techniques to expand and extend children's own language

◆ To understand the meanings, traditions, and heritage of their students and to articulate their legacy to local, national, and world history

◆ To understand the interaction between the students' culture and the prevailing school culture

Planning and Managing the Learning Environment

◆ To use knowledge of students' backgrounds and the dynamics of culture to organize the learning environment to promote students' physical, social, emotional, linguistic, artistic, intellectual, and cognitive development

◆ To establish and maintain supportive relationships among children from diverse backgrounds to promote positive self-concepts

- ◆ To initiate work routines, introduce subject matter, and offer educational tools and classroom exhibits that are appropriate to the children's age level, interests, language, and culture
- ◆ To plan, implement, and evaluate linguistically and culturally responsive and developmentally appropriate experiences that advance all areas of children's learning
- ◆ To plan for instruction in the native language and in English, as appropriate, and to manage dual-language instruction and transitions between languages
- ◆ To know how to stimulate social interaction among children from diverse cultural and linguistic backgrounds
- ◆ To develop routines to help children connect events and language(s)

Instruction and Assessment

To support the uniqueness of each child through the recognition of patterns of development, as well as family and cultural influences

- ◆ To use strategies that support native-language development
- ◆ To use strategies that promote the acquisition of English as a second language, as appropriate
- ◆ To implement a well-conceptualized and sequential curriculum that includes content, examples, and realistic images of diverse groups
- ◆ To use strategies that engage students in meaningful activities in the native language and in English, as appropriate
- ◆ To offer a variety of learning alternatives that reflect individual differences in language and culture, learning competencies, cognitive styles, interest, and the needs of students so as to reduce the conflict between individual and group needs
- ◆ To recognize that the same content may have different meanings to different groups of children when it is viewed through their distinct linguistic and cultural lenses
- ◆ To obtain, adapt, or create materials and resources that are relevant to students' language(s) and culture(s)
- ◆ To relate the children's knowledge to what is expected in school in ways that build on, rather than replace, their experiences in the home and community
- ◆ To use strategies that incorporate the home language and culture
- ◆ To make reading and writing, in both the native language and in English, appealing and significant by encouraging students to write about people, places, or activities that are important to them

- To provide opportunities for meaningful social and academic language use and interaction in both the native language and in English, as appropriate
- To use a variety of methods to promote individual development, meaningful social and academic language use, and interaction in both the native language and in English, as appropriate
- To use a variety of methods to promote individual development, meaningful learning, and group functioning in ways that accommodate students' skills, abilities, languages, and cultures
- To assess the competencies of each child by using a variety of formal and informal assessment procedures, including tests, anecdotal records, and work samples, recognizing the potential linguistic and cultural biases of existing assessment instruments and procedures
- To use assessment results for the purpose of prescribing culturally responsive individualized instructional programs for students with differing degrees of native-language and English proficiencies
- To model effective communication in the native language and in English and to use strategies that help children develop and expand their own speech and language skills

Collaboration and Professional and Ethical Practices

- To create and maintain collaborative, supportive relationships with parents, including the ability to communicate with them in their dominant language or to effectively use interpreters to enhance communication
- To work with parents and families to support children's learning and development in the native language and in English as a second language
- To actively involve parents and families in early learning programs and settings, using them as valuable linguistic and cultural resources in the teaching and learning process
- To work with families to determine their expectations for their children's native-language and English-language development
- To demonstrate ethical professional behavior requiring the self-examination of cultural perspective and biases and their potential inhibition of effective relationships with students and their families
- To support the home and community by embracing the values of bilingualism and cultural diversity in school programs
- To explain the role of the native language in children's development and the importance of supporting home and school interventions designed to enhance native-language and English as a second language acquisition
- To reinforce the importance of the native language in children's development and to provide support to maintain and preserve the native language

- To reinforce families' cultural and linguistic values
- To support school activities relating to the home and community
- To advocate quality child care services that provide opportunities to develop and maintain both the native language and English
- To contribute to the development, implementation, and evaluation of policies to improve early childhood programs for English-language learners

Note: Some competencies are appropriate to several of the categories; however, each is presented only once.

How Parents and Teachers Can Aid Students In Learning about the Sounds of Spoken Language

Teacher   Preschool   Early Childhood Education
                             Elementary School   Early Literacy Development
                                                       Family Engagement
                                                       Professional Development

The term for the ability to notice and work with the sounds in language is *phonological awareness.* Young children who have phonological awareness notice, for example, when words begin or end with the same sound—that *bag, ball,* and *bug* all begin with the sound of *b*; that words rhyme; and that sentences are made up of separate words. Research shows that the speed at which children learn to read often depends on how much phonological awareness they have when they begin kindergarten.

It is important for young children to be able to do the following:
  ♦ Repeat rhyming songs and poems, identify rhymes, and generate rhyming words when playing a rhyming game
  ♦ Recognize common sounds at the beginning of a series of words (alliteration)
  ♦ Isolate the beginning sounds in familiar words

Here are some things that you can do to help children learn about the sounds of spoken language:
  ♦ Choose books to read aloud that focus on sounds, rhyming, and alliteration.
  ♦ Have the children sing or say a familiar nursery rhyme or song. Repeat it several times, raising your voice on words that rhyme. Then have the children say the rhyming words with you.
  ♦ Invite the children to make up new verses for familiar songs or rhymes by changing the beginning sounds of words.
  ♦ Play word games with children. When possible, use children's names in the games.

Early Literacy Development

Early interventions to help low-achieving students improve their reading and writing skills establish the necessary foundation for effective learning in all other subjects. The following tools are included in this chapter:

What Does A Compact for Reading Look Like? excerpted from *A Compact for Reading Guide*, an activity of the Partnership for Family Involvement in Education, a joint project of the U.S. Department of Education, Corporation for National Service, Los Angeles Times Reading by 9, and Little Planet Learning.

How Teachers Can Put the School's Compact for Reading into Action, adapted from *A Compact for Reading Guide*, an activity of the Partnership for Family Involvement in Education, a joint project of the U.S. Department of Education, Corporation for National Service, Los Angeles Times Reading by 9, and Little Planet Learning.

What Does a Compact for Reading Look Like?

Administrator   All Grade Levels   Early Childhood Education
Counselor   Early Literacy Development
Special Educator   Family Engagement
Teacher   Professional Development

In 1998, the U.S. Department of Education developed a variety of *compacts for reading*. According to its guidelines, "A compact for reading is a written agreement among a partnership among families, principals, teachers, students and members of the wider outside community that describes how each partner can help improve the reading and other language arts skills of children from kindergarten through third grade, including those with disabilities and with limited English proficiency."

We, the _____ school community, establish this compact for reading to foster the improvement of reading and other language arts and to support the success of our students so that all may read well and independently. We believe this can be done with the planned partnership of parents, families, students, teachers, principals, and community members.

Parents' and Family's Responsibilities

We will:

♦ Make sure that our child attends school regularly, is on time, is prepared to learn, has his or her homework completed

♦ Know what skills our child is learning in reading and other language arts classes each day

♦ Do activities at home that continue our child's classroom learning at home

♦ Read with or to our child for 30 minutes each day, five days a week

♦ Get a library card for our child and encourage him or her to bring reading materials from the library into the home

♦ Attend parent–teacher conferences and communicate frequently with our child's teacher, through notes and conversation, about how well our child is doing

Student's Responsibilities

I will:

♦ Come to school on time and be ready to learn

♦ Pay attention to my teachers, family, and tutors and ask questions when I need help

♦ Ask my family to read to me or with me for 30 minutes each day, five days a week

♦ Complete my homework on time in a thorough and legible way

♦ Welcome help from my family on my homework and papers

♦ Return signed homework and papers to school

Teacher's Responsibilities

I will:

- ♦ Provide quality teaching and leadership to my students and their families
- ♦ Communicate frequently with families and tutors about my students' progress in reading and show how they can help
- ♦ Coordinate with other programs to make sure that nightly assignments do not exceed time limits
- ♦ Recognize that students are accountable for every assignment
- ♦ Participate in meaningful professional development in how to teach reading, how to communicate with families, and how to work with tutors
- ♦ Hold at least two parent–teacher conferences a year

Principal's Responsibilities

I will:

- ♦ Set high standards in reading and other language arts by providing a challenging curriculum
- ♦ Report publicly on schoolwide reading scores and help teachers and parents understand how adopting high standards can lead to the improvement of scores
- ♦ Allocate resources to ensure that high standards are met
- ♦ Hold workshops on standards in reading and ways to set the standards into practice at school and home
- ♦ Provide reading materials and training so that parents can help their children learn to read
- ♦ Establish training workshops for tutors and families to work with children on home activities
- ♦ Provide special benefits to teachers who meet with families and tutors in extended-learning programs
- ♦ Welcome and involve all families, especially those with low literacy skills or limited English proficiency or those who have not been involved in the school before

Community Member's Responsibilities

I will:

- ♦ Make a commitment to help all children learn to read
- ♦ Keep informed about the reading standards and performance of schools in my area
- ♦ Find out more about my school's literacy and reading standards
- ♦ Contact businesses and other community organizations that can donate resources to local schools to help them meet high standards in reading

- ◆ Volunteer to tutor students who need help in reading and other language arts skills or support and participate in training for tutors and other partners
- ◆ Help to open other facilities where children can go after school to read with someone or do their homework
- ◆ Build a community network of concerned adults consisting of community leaders, journalists, and others who can help to discuss and publicize local literacy issues

How Teachers Can Put the School's Compact for Reading into Action

Teacher   All Grade Levels   Early Childhood Education
                                                       Early Literacy Development
                                                       Family Engagement
                                                       Professional Development

In 1998, the U.S. Department of Education developed a variety of *compacts for reading*. According to its guidelines, "A compact for reading is a written agreement among a partnership among families, principals, teachers, students and members of the wider outside community that describes how each partner can help improve the reading and other language arts skills of children from kindergarten through third grade, including those with disabilities and with limited English proficiency."

Teachers should answer the questions below to raise the reading achievement level of their students.

- ♦ Do you regularly teach to the reading standards of the school, district, state, and federal government ?
- ♦ Do you send home learning activities that parents can use to reinforce classroom learning three to five times a week?
- ♦ Do you check to see whether students completed the activities and follow up when students fail to turn them in?
- ♦ Do you use student performance on home activities to guide classroom reading instruction?
- ♦ Do you encourage parents to read with their children 30 minutes a day and to get their children library cards?
- ♦ Do you send home monthly calendars to inform parents of the reading skills their children will be learning on a weekly or daily basis?
- ♦ Have you helped to set up extended-learning programs in your school for children who need the most help in reading?
- ♦ Have you lead or participated in training sessions for families as well as volunteer tutors in the community?
- ♦ Do you expect children to perform at basic and then increasingly advanced levels of reading in your classroom?
- ♦ Do you link classroom instruction with after-school and summer reading programs?
- ♦ Do you communicate regularly with parents of your students by telephone, notes, or e-mail messages?

Mentoring and Tutoring

Mentoring is a caring, supportive one-on-one relationship between a mentor and a mentee that is based on trust. Tutoring, also a one-on-one activity, focuses on academics and is an effective practice for addressing specific needs such as reading, writing, or math competencies. The following tools are included in this chapter:

How to Establish a Mentoring Program, developed by J. Eileene Welker, MS, CFCS, Assistant Professor, Ohio State University, Tuscarawas County Extension; 419 16th Street SW, New Philadelphia, OH 44663-6403, 330/339-2337, welker.2@osu.edu.

Mentoring Program Policy and Form Types, developed by Joan M. Reid, CFLE, Extension Agent, Family and Consumer Sciences, North Carolina State University, North Carolina Cooperative Extension, Granville County Center; P.O. Box 926, 208 Wall Street, Oxford, NC 27565, 919-603-1350, joan_reid@ncsu.edu.

How to Recruit, Screen, and Train Volunteers, excerpted from "Volunteers to Help Teachers and Schools Address Barriers to Learning," Center for Mental Health in Schools, Box 951563, Los Angeles, CA 9095-1563. The center is codirected by Howard Adelman and Linda Taylor and operates under the auspices of the School Mental Health Project in the Department of Psychology, University of California, Los Angeles. Permission granted.

How To Establish a Mentoring Program

Administrator   All Grade Levels   Mentoring and Tutoring
Teacher   Professional Development
                                                                     School–Community Collaboration

Establishing a mentoring program takes time, effort, and thought. The following material shows how to establish a program, how to market and recruit mentors, and how to prepare mentors.

Implementing a Mentoring Program

Thorough Planning Is Essential

The decision to start a mentoring program should not be taken lightly. A good foundation is needed to support the program throughout difficult phases. A professional structural framework is essential for successful matches and to prevent mentees and mentors from feeling abandoned, which can result in feelings of hurt, disappointment, rejection, and anger. In addition, a strong collaborative foundation can help to weather the ups and downs of conducting the program.

You will want to ensure that the agency or case manager performing the case-management duties has sufficient time to devote to the caseload. When the supervision of matches is compromised, mentors and mentees will not have their needs met, and issues needing attention within the matches can cause relationships to flounder. Careful case management is critical for a successful program that documents change in the clientele and is accountable to funding sources and the community.

Some Tasks for Starting a Mentoring Program

- Form and use a community coalition to help plan and implement.
- Conduct a community needs assessment.
- Set program philosophy, mission, goals, and objectives.
- Identify and hire a program coordinator or caseworker.
- Secure funding or other resources. You may need to write grants or plan periodic fund-raisers.
- Publicize the program.
- Recruit, screen, and select mentors (including performing background checks).
- Identify mentor-training facilitators.
- Organize training.
- Conduct and evaluate the training.
- Obtain liability insurance for volunteers.

- Recruit, screen, and select mentees.
- Conduct home assessments.
- Match mentees with mentors and introduce them.
- Provide support and activities for mentees and support and continuing education for mentors.
- Provide case management for all matches.
- Assess for closure.
- Evaluate match effectiveness periodically and at match closure.
- Develop a plan for sharing results with stakeholders.

Marketing and Recruitment

Recruiting mentors can be a challenging task. Marketing may illicit calls from interested persons. However, the long process of screening, training, and matching often loses many potential mentors. The following method, developed through trial and error, has led to a much higher percentage of interested callers becoming matched mentors.

- Radio public service announcements, with an emphasis on families needing a friend and the limited amount of time required per month, bring many more inquiries.
- The case manager sets up appointments to talk with interested individuals when they call for more information. Formerly, inquiring persons each were sent a brochure and packet of information to be filled out and returned if they were interested. A low percentage returned the application.
- At the first appointment with a potential mentor, the case manager explains the program and how it benefits families. This usually "hooks" the volunteer. The case manager also asks what motivated the person to consider being a mentor and what her or his expectations are. The case manager uses this information in making matches. The case manager also conducts the initial screening and paperwork at this time. Streamlining the paperwork to get only the necessary information once decreases the time devoted to screening. He or she then sets an appointment for a follow-up home visit.
- Training is set to accommodate the mentors' time schedules as much as possible.

Marketing Strategies

- Interviews with successful matches on radio and local cable television and in newspapers
- Articles and ads in all media
- Public service announcements on the radio, read by advisory committee members

♦ Posters with pictures of mentors, mentees, and children that contain information about program
♦ Brochures
♦ Promotion of the program to other agencies through brochures and speakers bureau
♦ Video showing interviews with mentors and mentees, to be shown at group presentations to raise money or solicit volunteers
♦ Magnet with program logo and address given to agencies and individuals
♦ Recruitment by case manager, staff, and advisory council
♦ Parades featuring a float with parents, mentors, and children wearing logo t-shirts. who distribute bookmarks with information to crowd

Preparing Mentors to Serve

Training mentors before they serve is important to better equip them to meet the needs of the mentees and to adequately prepare them for the challenges they will face. Training teaches mentors or reminds them of the important interpersonal skills required and helps them better understand young people. It also encourages the development of relationships between the mentors.

Steps for Organizing Training

♦ Have mentors complete the screening process before inclusion in training.
♦ Determine training objectives.
♦ Decide on the topics to include and identify a curriculum or write a training guide. There likely will not be enough time to cover all desired topics.
♦ Decide on and gather resource materials for the mentors.
♦ Invite community agency personnel to speak to the mentors.
♦ Use a variety of teaching methods to maintain interest and promote interaction
  • Small- and large-group discussion
  • Activities and role playing
  • Case studies
  • Brainstorming
  • Assigned reading between training sessions
♦ Maintain an informal atmosphere and include refreshments.

Suggested Topics for Training Mentors of Young Parents

♦ Philosophy, mission, and values of the program
♦ Mentor's personal goals
♦ Role of the mentor and qualities of effective mentors

- Match relationship
- Adolescent and early adult development
- Characteristics of adolescent parents
- Role of a nonresident father in a baby's life
- Young parents' extended families
- Poverty
- Cultural influences, as appropriate, such as Appalachian, Hispanic, etc.
- Self-esteem—parent and child
- Relationship building: trust, empathy, communication, and encouragement
- Stress management
- Parenting skills
- Problem-solving and decision-making skills
- Prenatal and postnatal care, labor and delivery, and postpartum depression
- Reproductive health, birth control, and sexually transmitted diseases
- Infant care, immunizations, communicable diseases, child sicknesses, and child abuse
- Case management and program requirements
- Pre- and post-training self-assessments
- Evaluation of training

Mentoring Program Policy and Form Types

Administrator   All Grade Levels   Mentoring and Tutoring
Teacher

Developing and using appropriate policies and forms helps to maintain the integrity of the mentoring program and the matches. As the program is being developed, care and time should be taken to create enforceable policies that will determine the daily operation of the program. Adherence to detailed policies provides an avenue for dealing with challenges, such as mentor and mentee applicants who are inappropriate for the program or who fail to support the program's goals and guidelines.

Below are some types of program policies that mentoring programs may want to develop in the planning stages. Policies should reflect the needs of the individual program.

Policies	Purpose	Need	Have	Don't Need
Program director position description	Describes the scope and duties of the program director position			
Case manager position description	Describes the scope and duties of the case manager position			
Mentor position description	Describes the expectations and limitations of volunteers serving as mentors, including time, money, and safety concerns			
Mentee position description	Describes the expectations and responsibilities of the mentees to the mentoring process			
Inquiry policy	Procedure to address inquiries from prospective mentors and mentees regarding the program			
Mentor eligibility criteria	Stipulates the program policy regarding eligibility for mentors to be accepted into the program			
Mentor intake policy	Procedure for intake of mentors accepted into the program, including background check, home assessment, etc.			

Policies	*Purpose*	*Need*	*Have*	*Don't Need*
Mentee family eligibility criteria	Stipulates the program policy regarding eligibility of prospective mentees and mentee families			
Mentee family intake policy	Procedure for intake of mentee families accepted into the program			
Match determination policy	Procedure and considerations for matching mentors with mentees			
Match process policy	Procedure for introducing mentor and mentee			
Match ground rules	Program ground rules and guidelines to be shared with mentors and mentees at match time for clarification of expectations			
Match supervision policy	Procedures for case management of the matches including assessment and documentation of match progress			
Match closure policy	Policy for determination of need and procedure for closing matches			
Case manager, mentor, and mentee reports on the match	Evaluation tools to gather information from the case manager, mentors, and mentees on the effectiveness of the match and identify challenges			

The following are suggested types of case management forms that will make it easier to ensure that policies are followed and adequate information is gathered and on file. Close attention to such details adds credibility to the program and protects the program, program personnel, mentors, and mentees. Full documentation is needed to deal effectively with problems that may develop, possible legal involvement, and case manager turnover.

Form	Purpose	Need	Have	Don't Need
Application forms	Application to be a mentor or a mentee			
Mentor and mentee interview guides	Record of necessary information during the mentor and mentee interview process			
Home assessment interview	Record completed during mentor home assessment			
Reference form and cover letter	Form sent to references for volunteer applicants to complete and return to case manager			
Case plan	Written goals and strategies for the mentee			
Case termination	Written record of closure, including reasons and recommendations regarding potential future involvement in the program			
Confidentiality form	Mentor's agreement to maintain confidentiality			
Personal auto verification	Verification of auto liability insurance coverage for employees and volunteers			
Inquiry forms (mentor and mentee)	Documentation of personal information and actions taken when potential mentors or mentees inquire about participating in the program.			
Match plan	Worksheet for case manager to document rationale for the match and areas to monitor during the match			
Mentee consent form	Mentee's indication of voluntary participation; may or may not choose to have information and pictures used in program promotional efforts			
Emergency medical authorization	Authorization for medical treatment for mentee (if a minor) and mentee's children			
Matching preferences	Information regarding mentor and mentee preferences to assist case manager in making compatible matches			

Form	Purpose	Need	Have	Don't Need
Goal sheet/ mentor contact form	Forms for recording progress toward mentee goals and substance of mentor and mentee meetings			
Mentee family profile	Snapshot evaluation of mentee family—ability to adhere to program policy, needs, and challenges, personal data, and other info			
Mentee match information	Personal information about the mentee that can be shared with the mentor			

Source: Joan Reid, MS, CFLE, Ohio State University Extension, and the Side by Side Family Mentoring Program, Big Brothers Big Sisters (with permission), Coshocton County, Ohio, 2003.

Qualities of Effective Mentors

Although we think of mentors as being nice people, more is required of them. If the program goals are to encourage positive changes in the mentees, then mentors need to be at their best. There are some personal characteristics that help mentors to be effective with their mentees. Here are some characteristics that were identified by mentors in the Side by Side Family Mentoring Program in Coshocton County, Ohio:

- Patient
- Tolerant
- Understanding
- Compassionate
- Nonjudgmental
- Good listener
- Caring
- Kind
- Honest and trustworthy
- Approachable
- Accepting
- Sets Limits
- Loyal
- Good at motivating and encouraging
- Fun
- Outgoing
- Positive attitude
- Nurturing
- Supportive
- Perseverant
- Firm
- Available
- Dependable
- Punctual
- Responsible
- Straightforward or down-to-earth
- Positive role model

How To Recruit, Screen, and Train Volunteers

Administrator   All Grade Levels   Mentoring and Tutoring
Teacher   Professional Development
                                                                 School–Community Collaboration

The Center for Mental Health in Schools publishes a series of superb online resources for educational and health professionals. For a complete list, visit their Web site, http:// smph.psych.ucla.edu.

Properly trained volunteers are a great help in minimizing disruptions and reengaging errant students. When a teacher has trained a volunteer to focus on designated students, the volunteer knows what to watch for and can move quickly at the first indication that the student needs special guidance and support.

Recruitment

To make the effort worthwhile, recruit a minimum of nine hours of volunteer time per week (e.g., three volunteers each giving three hours a week). Sources include the following:

- ♦ Parent volunteers: Because of their special interest and proximity, recruiting parents may be the best place to begin.
- ♦ School volunteers: In many locales, student volunteers are a good source, especially those from local universities, occupational centers, etc. In addition, some high school students can be recruited (e.g., from private prep schools, classes for pregnant teenagers, or continuation schools).
- ♦ Community volunteers: Subsequently, recruitment can focus on expanding to community volunteer organizations and to senior citizen groups.

The following general steps can be used to recruit volunteers:

- ♦ Identify specific sources of volunteers. Ask individuals who are familiar with local resources and look through reference materials, including local phone directories.
- ♦ Make initial calls to determine programs and persons who may provide access to potential volunteers. For example, check with the school principal for the names of the PTA president and other parent leaders; get the names of university and college faculty who teach courses involving a practicum (e.g., contact departments of education, psychology, social work, and child development programs, as well as field work offices; call high schools, continuation schools, and occupational programs for the names of counselors, principals, and teachers; or call an association of retired citizens.
- ♦ Call specific offices and persons to explain the project and opportunities for volunteer participation.

- Send written information, including flyers that can be posted.
- Send out volunteer coordinators to provide additional information. If possible, presentations should be made directly to potential volunteers (e.g., during classes or special meetings).
- Schedule regular, ongoing contact by volunteer coordinators. For example, to keep high visibility, the volunteer coordinators should continue to post flyers and make presentations.

Screening and Placement

- Screening: Brief interviews can be conducted to explain the program and determine whether the volunteer understands and is willing to commit to the time and goals of the endeavor. Information about previous experience and career interests can help to identify the best applicants.
- Placement: If more than one teacher or staff member is participating in the program, placement involves making judgments about how well a volunteer's interests and experiences match a specific classroom teacher or population.

Service Learning

Service learning connects meaningful community service experiences with academic learning. This teaching and learning method promotes personal and social growth, career development, and civic responsibility, and it can be a powerful vehicle for effective school reform at all grade levels. The following tools are included in this chapter:

What Is Service Learning and What Are Its Benefits? developed by Franklin P. Schargel.

What Are the Benefits of Effective Service Learning Programs? excerpted from the Corporation for National and Community Service, Students in Service to America, Washington, DC, 2002; www.usafreedomcorps.gov.

How to Bring Service Learning into Classrooms, excerpted from the Corporation for National and Community Service, Students in Service to America, Washington, DC, 2002; www.usafreedomcorps.gov.

What Are the Hallmarks of Effective Service Learning Programs? excerpted from the Corporation for National and Community Service, Students in Service to America, Washington, DC, 2002; www.usafreedomcorps.gov.

What Is Service Learning and What Are Its Benefits?

Administrator   All Grade Levels   Alternative Schooling
Teacher   Career and Technical Education
School-Community Collaboration
Service Learning

What Is Service Learning?

♦ Service learning combines community service with academic instruction and develops critical thinking, employability skills, expertise in various subjects, and civic responsibility.

♦ Service learning is a method whereby students learn and develop through active participation in thoughtfully organized service that is conducted in and meets the needs of communities.

♦ Service learning is coordinated with an elementary school, secondary school, institution of higher education, or community service program and the community.

♦ Service learning helps to foster civic responsibility.

♦ Service learning is integrated with and enhances the academic curriculum of the students or the education components of the community service program in which the participants are enrolled.

♦ Service learning provides structured time for students or participants to reflect on the service experience.

What Do Service Learning Programs Do?

♦ Provide training and support to students, faculty, staff, and community participants

♦ Develop service learning partnerships with community organizations, employers, and governmental organizations

♦ Provide students with transferable employability skills

♦ Provide students with educational credits for their service learning experiences.

What Are the Benefits of Service Learning?

- Makes curriculum relevant to students' daily lives
- Builds a sense of community responsibility
- Develops problem-solving skills
- Builds career awareness

How Does Service Learning Benefits Teachers?

- Connects course content material to the outside world of work
- Validates the curriculum
- Engages learners in the subject matter
- Enhances communication with the community

What Are the Key Components of Service Learning?

- Link to in-school course competencies
- Relevant assignments with
  - Clear objectives and evaluation criteria
  - Critical thinking and problem solving
  - Reflection and evaluation
- Meaningful contributions to the community

How Does It Work?

- School staff provide support and practical suggestions to interested faculty, students, and community representatives.
- Students and faculty design a service program with business representatives tailored to the needs of the student, school, curriculum, and business partner.
- Students implement their program over the course of one or more terms.
- Students reflect on their experience and how it related to course objectives through class presentations, papers, or other means.

What Are the Benefits
of Effective Service Learning Programs?

Administrator   Middle School   Alternative Schooling
Teacher   High School   Career and Technical Education
                                             School-Community Collaboration
                                                           Service Learning

Studies suggest that schools with well-designed service and service learning programs can provide a number of benefits for students, teachers, schools, after-school programs, and communities.

Increased Student Engagement

Students who participate in high-quality service learning programs can become more active learners. Service learning allows students to make the critical connection between the knowledge they are acquiring in the classroom and its use in the real world. Through service learning, students are taught to think critically, make key decisions, interact with others, and provide service that makes a difference, both to themselves and to the community. As a result, their school attendance and motivation to learn can increase.

Improved Academic Achievement

When teachers explicitly tie service activities to academic standards and learning objectives, students can show gains on measures of academic achievement, including standardized tests. Service learning that includes environmental activities, for example, can help students to apply math skills (such as measurement and problem solving) and science skills (such as prediction and knowledge of botany) if they are explicitly woven into the experience.

Improved Thinking Skills

Service learning helps students to improve their ability to analyze complex tasks, draw inferences from data, solve new problems, and make decisions. The degree to which improvements occur in these higher-order thinking skills depends on how well teachers can get students to talk about and understand the service activities they are performing.

Improved Character

Service learning promotes responsibility, trustworthiness, and caring for others. Through service projects, students learn not to let each other down or to disappoint those being served. Young people who participate in service learning acquire an ethic of service, volunteer more frequently, and say they plan to continue to volunteer as they get older.

Improved Social Behavior

Young people who are active in service programs are less likely to engage in risky behaviors. For many young people, service learning provides a venue in which they can be more successful than they have been in more traditional classroom settings. Service learning also can reinforce the kinds of social behaviors that are crucial for success in the workforce.

Stronger Ties to Schools, Communities, and Society

Service learning can give students a sense of belonging and responsibility for their communities. For example, through service projects, young people often come to believe they can make a difference in their schools, communities, and society. Some studies have established a strong connection between this sense of efficacy and academic achievement, as well as greater concern for personal health and well-being.

Exposure to New Careers

Through service learning, many students come into contact with adults in careers that otherwise would remain hidden to them. For example, students may meet social workers, scientists, park rangers, government workers, health workers, and others who work in community agencies. By assisting them and seeing how schoolwork relates to what they do, students can acquire higher or more varied career or job aspirations, along with a more realistic understanding of what is necessary to attain them.

Positive School Environments

When service learning is practiced schoolwide, program experience shows that teachers can feel reinvigorated, the dialogue on teaching and learning can be stimulated, and the school climate can improve. In fact, many teachers become advocates for incorporating more service into the curriculum. Service learning programs also have been associated with reduced negative student behaviors and disciplinary referrals, as well as engagement of at-risk students and lower dropout rates.

Stronger Community Groups

When young people form early connections with community groups through service activities, the groups themselves are often the beneficiaries. Young people can infuse a charity or civic group with energy and inspiration; become members of the volunteer force, staff, or board; help to build awareness of the group's mission throughout the community; and help an organization to garner positive press and media attention.

Increased Community Support for Schools

Community members who work with the young people engaged in service learning activities frequently say they come to view youth differently, seeing them as assets who contribute to the community in positive ways. Public support for schools can grow as a result of student involvement in community activities.

How To Bring Service Learning into Classrooms

Administrator   Middle School   Alternative Schooling
Teacher   High School   Career and Technical Education
                                            School-Community Collaboration
                                                  Service Learning

The following steps will help teachers to create an effective service project or service learning program. Although all of these steps are useful to consider, you may not need to perform then all or follow them in the order presented here. The planning and implementation of service and service learning programs are dynamic processes, and projects vary greatly. Read through all of the steps before undertaking your project, and remember to include young people in as many phases as possible.

Step 1: Assess the needs and resources of your community and school. In selecting a project, consult with community members, civic groups, businesses, government officials, school personnel, and students to determine the needs of your community and the available resources, including partnership opportunities.

Step 2: Form community partnerships. Most successful service projects require forming partnerships. You can build on existing relationships and connections, or you can develop new ones with the potential partners identified in Step 1. Be realistic about your resources, needs, and limitations, and make sure that your goals are of mutual interest to all partners. Also be concrete about the roles and responsibilities of each partner organization.

Step 3: Set specific educational goals and curriculum. Determine what you expect the young people to learn. Even service or service learning projects organized by community-based organizations or after-school programs should set specific educational goals. Establish what content objectives or standards will be addressed, and incorporate your service and learning objectives or standards into lesson plans. Devise ways to measure and assess whether those goals are being met, such as reflection and assessment activities. When evaluating student performance, assess students' effort and mastery of the subject. Service outcomes may not be what you expected.

Step 4: Select a project and begin preliminary planning. Pick a project and determine how all partners can work together to achieve the desired goals. Try to determine your human, financial, physical, and intellectual needs and whether you will need additional partners to provide the required resources. Be sure to identify people in your school or organization who can coordinate the project and maintain continuity from year to year.

Step 5: Plan your project in detail. Set up a timeline, create a budget, and assign tasks. Think about how to include your partners in this process. As with any project, thorough planning—including the creation of schedules, benchmarks, budgets, evaluation and assessment tools, and documentation can identify and correct many potential problems.

Step 6: Acquire the necessary funding and resources. If additional funds, goods, or services are needed, consider seeking assistance from local businesses, national corporations, parents, faith-based organizations, government programs (such as AmeriCorps, Senior Corps, Learn and Serve America, or your state education agency), civic groups, and other community organizations or sources of federal, state, and local funds.

Step 7: Implement and manage the project. Put your plan into action. Continually assess your project to determine what is working and what could be improved. Involve project partners in evaluating and improving your project.

Step 8: Organize reflection activities. Make sure students are thinking about their service experience on a regular basis (for example, through journals or classroom assignments) and organize activities that allow students to analyze their service and see how their ideas, knowledge, and perceptions are changing. Use such reflections to assess and improve the project. You may want to use the online or printable Record of Service found at www.usafreedomcorps.gov.

Step 9: Assess and evaluate your service program. Ensure that your evaluation assesses the outcomes of the service project for the youth, the community, and the organizations involved. Documentation and evaluation of the project will create a legacy for the individuals and the organizations who participated in and benefited from your service activities. It also will point the way to the next project for your classroom and may foster activities in other classrooms.

Step 10: Celebrate achievements. Everyone likes to be recognized for a job well done. Recognition of students can help to build habits of service and lead to a lifetime of community involvement. Don't forget to recognize key community partners as well. Recognition may include displays in school or online, celebratory events such as ribbon cuttings or groundbreakings, visits by local officials, and participation in national recognition programs.

What Are the Hallmarks
of Effective Service Learning Programs?

Administrator
Teacher

Middle School
High School

Alternative Schooling
Career and Technical Education
School-Community Collaboration
Service Learning

Service and service learning can be used to teach any subject and to meet a wide variety of community needs. However, to provide valuable service, build civic skills, and increase student achievement, project and program designers may wish to consider including some of the following practices that program experience has shown to be effective.

♦ Service activities should last a sustained or significant duration. Program experience suggests that a minimum of 40 hours over a school year is necessary to yield positive results for students and the community.

♦ Teacher or after-school program coordinators or sponsors need to work with students to draw the connections between what the students are doing and what they should be learning. Even if service activities are conducted outside class, it is important for the project to have clear and specific learning objectives.

♦ The service that students perform should have a strong connection to the curriculum they are studying or to their after-school activities.

♦ The relationship between service and democratic practices, ideas, and history should be made explicit so that students see service as a civic responsibility.

♦ Project participants should be given time to reflect on their service. This may involve asking students to keep a journal or having teachers and organizers lead discussions or coordinate activities that get participants to analyze and think critically about their service. These activities need to be planned, not left to chance.

♦ Students should have a role not only in executing the service project but also in making decisions about its development. Students should be involved in leadership roles during all phases of the project.

♦ To ensure that service is really useful and strengthens community ties, strong partnerships with community groups based on mutually agreed upon goals, roles, and responsibilities are essential.

♦ The most important feature of effective service and service learning programs is that both learning and service are emphasized. For example, students in quality service learning programs are graded on what they learn, just as they would be for any other class. But they also are expected to carry out service projects of genuine benefit to the community.

Alternative Schooling

Alternative schooling provides potential dropouts a variety of options that can lead to graduation. Programs pay special attention to the student's individual social needs and academic requirements for a high school diploma. The following tool is included in this chapter:

How to Plan, Develop, and Monitor and Alternative Education Contract, developed by Dr. Marie Sobers, Transition Coordinator for Alternative Education, and Dr. Renee Lacey, Supervisor of Alternative Education and Summer School, Prince William County Schools, Manassas, Virginia.

How To Plan, Develop, and Monitor an Alternative Education Contract

Administrator	Middle School	After-School Opportunities
Counselor	High School	Alternative Schooling
Special Educator		Professional Development
Teacher		Service Learning

Dr. Marie Sobers, transition coordinator for alternative education, and Dr. Renee Lacey, supervisor of alternative education and summer school, are professional educators working in the Prince William County Schools in Manassas, Virginia. They have developed a series of tools that help: to plan, develop, and monitor an alternative education contract. The items appear on the following pages.

Although each state's standards vary, this provides an excellent template.

Alternative Education Referral

The principal's signature verifies that the student is registered and meets the criteria for placement in alternative education and that the school will be responsible for payment (direct billing).

Signature _____ Title _____ Date _____

Date of referral _____ Resulting action _____ Date of action _____

Student _____

Date of birth _____ Age _____ Sex _____ Ethnic code _____

Grade _____ Grade(s) repeated _____

Student No. _____ School _____

School contact _____ Date of child study _____

Disability (none or category) _____

Parent or Guardian Information

Indicate primary contact

Name _____ Home phone _____ Work phone _____

Address _____

Relationship _____

Name _____ Home phone _____ Work phone _____

Address _____

Relationship _____

School and Agency Contacts

Provide name and telephone number

School guidance counselor

_____

School social worker

_____

Attendance officer

_____

Special education

_____

Social worker

_____

Court/probation

_____ _____

Family counselor/therapist

_____

FAPT services

_____

Medical professional

_____

Other

_____

Areas of Concern

Please indicate the level of concern: 0 = None; 1 = Mild; 2 = Moderate; 3 = Serious

- ☐ Academic concerns
- ☐ Breaking of rules
- ☐ Decline in quality of work
- ☐ Defiance of authority
- ☐ Depression, sadness
- ☐ Displays of anger
- ☐ Disruptive behavior in classroom
- ☐ Extreme negativism
- ☐ Frequent need for discipline
- ☐ Impaired memory

- ☐ Inattentiveness
- ☐ Lack of concentration
- ☐ Lack of motivation
- ☐ Obscene language, gestures
- ☐ Other concerns
- ☐ Sleeping in class
- ☐ Tardiness to class
- ☐ Verbal abuse
- ☐ Withdrawal, a loner, separateness

Summarize the reason for the referral; include the precipitating event, if appropriate:

Previous Interventions

- ☐ 504 plan
- ☐ Additional grading reports
- ☐ Anger management
- ☐ Appropriate course placement
- ☐ Attendance officer referral
- ☐ Behavior contracts
- ☐ Behavior-management system
- ☐ Behavior referred to administration
- ☐ CAFAS
- ☐ Challenge
- ☐ Child-specific team
- ☐ Child-study team
- ☐ Community volunteering
- ☐ Conflict management
- ☐ Course planning to graduation

- ☐ Daily behavior point sheets
- ☐ Detention
- ☐ FAPT
- ☐ Functional behavioral assessment
- ☐ Individual counseling
- ☐ In-school suspension
- ☐ Job Corps
- ☐ Local screening
- ☐ Medical evaluation
- ☐ Mentoring
- ☐ Out-of-school suspension
- ☐ Parent conference(s)
- ☐ Parent escort in school
- ☐ Parent liaison
- ☐ Parent meetings
- ☐ Parent orientation
- ☐ Parent phone calls
- ☐ Parenting classes
- ☐ Peer mediation

- ☐ Peer tutoring
- ☐ Positive reinforcement
- ☐ Review code of behavior
- ☐ Probation officer contact
- ☐ Referral to psychologist
- ☐ Referral to social worker
- ☐ Smoking-cessation classes
- ☐ Special education services provided
- ☐ Student conference(s) and feedback
- ☐ Substance abuse assessment
- ☐ Teacher or counselor team conference
- ☐ Time-out sessions
- ☐ Transition planning
- ☐ Vocational assessment
- ☐ Vocational counseling
- ☐ Work study

Interventions and Services Provided to the Child

Please summarize

Parent, guidance, administrative, and other involvement:

Special education (current and prior):

Medical concerns/medication:

Required Attachments

☐ Attendance summary
(two years if possible)

☐ Child study summary

☐ Discipline record (expanded summary
for two years, if possible)

☐ Documentation of prior serious
behavioral interventions (principal's
hearing, long-term suspension, etc.)

☐ Guidance contacts

☐ Most recent special education
involvement (documentation and
Individualized Education Plan)

☐ Outside agency contacts

☐ Parent contacts

☐ Test card data

☐ Transcript

Alternative Education Contract

_____ provides a continuum of services that focus on meeting the needs of each child so that his or her maximum potential will be realized. These services include but are not limited to those that address behavior, academic progress, work readiness, lifelong learning, and effective group participation so that individuals will become productive members of society.

The student named below has been selected to participate in the continuum of services beyond those offered by the base school. The success of the individualized program depends on the participation and cooperation of the student, staff, and parent or guardian. In addition to compliance with the _____ code of behavior, program participants and parents are expected to abide by the following conditions to ensure that each person is afforded the greatest benefits of the program.

- Participants will attend the program regularly and on time.
- Parent or guardian will contact the appropriate staff if the participant will be absent for any reason.
- Parent or guardian will communicate regularly with the program facilitator.
- Parent or guardian will cooperate with the program facilitator to appropriately address and correct inappropriate behavior during program hours.
- If either the participant or the parent or guardian cannot meet these stipulations, the child may no longer be able to participate in the service.

Service Provided

Student name	Student number	Provider	Course(s)	Begin date	End date

Our signatures below indicate our willingness to comply with the conditions as stated and gives permission for _____ to participate in Prince William County Schools Alternative Education Continuum of Services.

Student _____ Date _____

Parent or guardian _____ Date _____

Transition coordinator _____ Date _____

Alternative Education Plan

The student and facilitator plan this together. The *student* does the writing.

Name _____ SSN _____

Date of birth _____ Age _____ Base school _____ Grade _____

Parent or guardian _____

Home phone _____ Work phone (M) _____

Work phone (F) _____

Address _____

_____

Date written _____ Beginning date _____ Ending date _____

Student _____ Parent _____

Transition coordinator _____

Indicators of Need (Check all that apply)

□ Performs substantially below the performance level for pupils of the same age, as indicated by standardized testing □ Reading level □ Math level □ Language level	□ Concerns relating to or has been assessed as being chemically dependent
□ Is at least one year behind in satisfactorily completing coursework or obtaining credits for graduation	□ Previously received alternative education services
□ Exhibits oppositional and disruptive behaviors	□ Has been chronically truant
□ Discipline infractions have resulted in a contract or principal's hearing	□ Has an active Individualized Education Plan □ Disability

Comments:

Academic Goals

Goal _____

Short-term objectives	Specific strategies	Evaluation
Annual goal result: Date _____		

Goal _____

Short-term objectives	Specific strategies	Evaluation
Annual goal result: Date_____		

Goal _____

Short-term objectives	Specific strategies	Evaluation
Annual goal result: Date_____		

Goal _____

Short-term objectives	Specific strategies	Evaluation
Annual goal result: Date_____		

Goal _____

Short-term objectives	Specific strategies	Evaluation
Annual goal result: Date_____		

Behavioral and Social Goals

Goal _____

Short-term objectives	Specific strategies	Evaluation
Annual goal result: Date_____		

Goal _____

Short-term objectives	Specific strategies	Evaluation
Annual goal result: Date_____		

Goal _____

Short-term objectives	Specific strategies	Evaluation
Annual goal result: Date_____		

Goal _____

Short-term objectives	Specific strategies	Evaluation
Annual goal result: Date_____		

Transition Goals

Goal _____

Short-term objectives	Specific strategies	Evaluation
Annual goal result: Date_____		

Goal _____

Short-term objectives	Specific strategies	Evaluation
Annual goal result: Date_____		

Goal _____

Short-term objectives	Specific strategies	Evaluation
Annual goal result: Date_____		

Goal _____

Short-term objectives	Specific strategies	Evaluation
Annual goal result: Date_____		

After-School Opportunities

Many schools provide after-school and summer enhancement programs that eliminate information loss and inspire interest in a variety of areas. Such experiences are especially important for students who are at risk of school failure because they fill the afternoon "gap time" with constructive and engaging activities. The following tools are included in this chapter:

How Do I Start an After-School Program? developed by Angela King, Executive Director, Cannon County REACH Program; 612 Lehman Street, Woodbury, TN 37190, 615-563-5518.

What Are the Perceptions of a Community Experience Site Supervisor? Diana Spooner and Chad Eltjes, Des Moines Public Schools, 1800 Grand Avenue, Des Moines, IA 50309-3382, 515-242-7549.

How to Measure Staff's Perceptions of Their Students' Views of School and Community Service, Diana Spooner and Chad Eltjes, Des Moines Public Schools, 1800 Grand Avenue, Des Moines, IA 50309-3382, 515-242-7549.

How to Measure Parents' Perceptions of Their Children's Views of School and Community Service, Diana Spooner and Chad Eltjes, Des Moines Public Schools, 1800 Grand Avenue, Des Moines, IA 50309-3382, 515-242-7549.

How to Measure Students' Perceptions of School and Community Service, Diana Spooner and Chad Eltjes, Des Moines Public Schools, 1800 Grand Avenue, Des Moines, IA 50309-3382, 515-242-7549.

How Do I Start
an After-School Program?

Administrator   All Grade Levels   After-School Opportunities
Teacher   Alternative Schooling
                                                              Professional Development
                                                        School–Community Collaboration

Most after-school programs have not undergone extensive planning and development. The REACH (Reach for Enrichment and Community Health) program of Woodbury has, and it has agreed to share its process with the readers of this book.

Research your population using surveys.
- At risk
- Preschool
- Teenagers

List resources in your area.
- Stores
- Government
- School system
- Medical programs
- State programs

Design the program based on your particular area.
- Calendar
- Hours and days
- Schedule
- Transportation plan

Obtain funding.
- Grants (local, state, federal)
- Donations
- Fund-raising
- Partnerships
- In-kind donations

Hire staff.
- Director
- Tutors

Recruit children for the population you have targeted.
- Start small and expand
- Consider the budget
- Consider your geographic area

Identify areas of need.
- Nutrition
- Academics (math, reading, homework)
- Enrichment
- Weekends
- Summer
- Parent programs
- Intervention
- Remediation
- Staff development

Evaluate the program.
- Data collection
- Pre- and post-tests
- Surveys

What Are the Perceptions of a Community Experience Site Supervisor?

Administrator	Middle School	After-School Opportunities
Teacher	High School	Family Engagement
		School–Community Collaboration
		Service Learning

To reduce the number of suspensions and to increase the graduation rate, the Des Moines Public Schools established the Community Service Project. It links the community, school, and family to develop a sense of connection for students. Students who otherwise may be excluded from school by suspensions or expulsions are provided the opportunity to continue their education program with enriched experience in applying their skills to real-life experiences. Students are referred through the school district's expulsion process or by disciplinary action as a result of multiple suspensions.

Community Experience Site Supervisor

Student _____ Site supervisor _____

Site _____ Date _____

What were your first impressions of the student?

What changes were noticeable in the student?
For example, being on time, attendance, attitude, work ethic, etc.

Conversations with the student:

Suggestions for the student:

Positive interactions with the student:

Negative interactions with the student:

What would you consider to be the student's strengths?

What would you consider to be the student's weaknesses?

Do you feel the student's attitude toward school has changed?   How?

How did the student interact with his or her co-workers?

Other comments:
Would you take another student?   Yes   No

How To Measure Staff's Perceptions
of Their Students' Views
# of School and Community Service

Administrator	Middle School	After-School Opportunities
Counselor	High School	Family Engagement
Teacher		School–Community Collaboration
		Service Learning

To reduce the number of suspensions and to increase the graduation rate, the Des Moines Public Schools established the Community Service Project. It links the community, school, and family to develop a sense of connection for students. Students who otherwise may be excluded from school by suspensions or expulsions are provided the opportunity to continue their education program with enriched experience in applying their skills to real-life experiences. Students are referred through the school district's expulsion process or by disciplinary action as a result of multiple suspensions. The following survey is distributed to staff.

Date_____

Your Name _____ Student's Name _____

Please indicate your perception of how this student feels about the following:

	Positive_____Negative				
Attending school	1	2	3	4	5
Participating in a community service project	1	2	3	4	5
Completing homework on time	1	2	3	4	5
Earning a god grade at school	1	2	3	4	5
Helping someone with a need	1	2	3	4	5
Following school rules and policies	1	2	3	4	5
Accomplishing a school goal	1	2	3	4	5
Getting along with other students at school	1	2	3	4	5
Getting along with adults at school	1	2	3	4	5
Participating in your community	1	2	3	4	5

How To Measure Parents' Perceptions of Their Children's Views of School and Community Service

Administrator	Middle School	After-School Opportunities
Counselor	High School	Family Engagement
Teacher		School–Community Collaboration
		Service Learning

To reduce the number of suspensions and to increase the graduation rate, the Des Moines Public Schools established the Community Service Project. It links the community, school, and family to develop a sense of connection for students. Students who otherwise may be excluded from school by suspensions or expulsions are provided the opportunity to continue their education program with enriched experience in applying their skills to real-life experiences. Students are referred through the school district's expulsion process or by disciplinary action as a result of multiple suspensions. The following survey is distributed to parents.

Date _____

Your Name _____ Student's Name _____

Please indicate your perception of how your son or daughter feels about the following:

	Positive_____Negative				
Attending school	1	2	3	4	5
Participating in a community service project	1	2	3	4	5
Completing homework on time	1	2	3	4	5
Earning a good grade at school	1	2	3	4	5
Helping someone with a need	1	2	3	4	5
Following school rules and policies	1	2	3	4	5
Accomplishing a school goal	1	2	3	4	5
Getting along with other students at school	1	2	3	4	5
Getting along with adults at school	1	2	3	4	5
Participating in your community	1	2	3	4	5

How To Measure Students' Perceptions
of School and Community Service

Administrator	Middle School	After-School Opportunities
Counselor	High School	Family Engagement
Teacher		School–Community Collaboration
		Service Learning

To reduce the number of suspensions and to increase the graduation rate, the Des Moines Public Schools established the Community Service Project. It links the community, school, and family to develop a sense of connection for students. Students who otherwise may be excluded from school by suspensions or expulsions are provided the opportunity to continue their education program with enriched experience in applying their skills to real-life experiences. Students are referred through the school district's expulsion process or by disciplinary action as a result of multiple suspensions. The following survey is distributed to students.

Date _____

Your Name _____ Student's Name _____

Please indicate your perception of how your son or daughter feels about the following:

	Positive				Negative
Attending school	1	2	3	4	5
Participating in a community service project	1	2	3	4	5
Completing homework on time	1	2	3	4	5
Earning a good grade at school	1	2	3	4	5
Helping someone with a need	1	2	3	4	5
Following school rules and policies	1	2	3	4	5
Accomplishing a school goal	1	2	3	4	5
Getting along with other students at school	1	2	3	4	5
Getting along with adults at school	1	2	3	4	5
Participating in your community	1	2	3	4	5

Professional Development

Teachers who work with youth at high risk of academic failure need to feel supported and need an avenue by which they can continue to develop skills and techniques and learn about innovative strategies. The following tools are included in this chapter:

How to Identify High-Performing At-Risk Students, from the *Handbook for Identification of Hispanic Gifted and Talented Bilingual Students,* published by the New York City Board of Education, Office of Bilingual Education, 1984.

How Do You Measure the Effectiveness of Your Professional Development? developed by Tom Krubs, Chair, Kansas Learning First Alliance; 1420 SW Arrowhead Road, Topeka, KS 66604, www.teachkansas.org.

How to Plan for Successful Staff Development, from *The Principal as Instructional Leader* by Sally J. Zepeda Eye on Education, 2003, pp. 69–70. Used with the permission of the publisher.

Checklist for Running Good Staff Meetings, developed by Franklin P. Schargel.

How To Identify High-Performing At-Risk Students

Counselor   All Grade Levels   Alternative Schooling
Teacher   Individualized Instruction
                                                                 Professional Development

When educators are asked about at-risk students, they frequently see all at-risk students as low-performing students. Yet many of our at-risk students are high-achieving gifted and talented students who are bored by the lack of challenging opportunities posed in traditional classrooms. Teachers and counselors can help to identify gifted and talented at-risk students by using the following survey.

Teacher Checklist

Student's name _____ Date _____

School _____ Class _____ Age _____

Teacher or person completing this form _____

How long have you known this child?_____

Please check the items that describe this child:

- ☐ Asks many questions, sometimes too many and sometime very difficult ones
- ☐ Sees humor in situations
- ☐ Is able to laugh at self and sometimes laughs at others
- ☐ Uses things in unique ways and sees multiple uses for things
- ☐ Mixes elements (two languages, two concepts, two ideas) to create new words, concepts, or ideas
- ☐ Becomes obsessed with exploring a specific topic of interest
- ☐ Initiates his or her own projects
- ☐ Has a specific interest and is knowledgeable in specific area (s)
- ☐ Is preoccupied with his or her own interests
- ☐ Has less difficulty making decisions than other students
- ☐ Will not stop an activity until satisfied.
- ☐ Likes to memorize things, remembers trivia
- ☐ Remembers the details of class events, trips, and occurrences in school
- ☐ Rapidly acquires language skills
- ☐ Learns by reasoning things out by him- or herself; sees logical and commonsense answers
- ☐ Enjoys difficult and challenging tasks

□ Is knowledgeable in many subjects or topics

□ Finds many ways of understanding complicated material

□ Places emphasis on including many details in his or her work

□ Transfers knowledge from one area to another by picking out important ideas, facts, and details

□ Is sensitive to the needs and feelings of classmates

□ Has his or her own opinions and ideas and maintains them in the face of opposition

□ Does not accept what he or she perceives as unfair or illogical

□ Is able to influence the group, openly or unobtrusively

This student belongs in a special program for gifted students because:

Signature of teacher_____

How Do You Measure the Effectiveness
of Your Professional Development?

Administrator	All Grade Levels	Professional Development
Teacher		Safe Learning Environments
		School–Community Collaboration

The Kansas Learning First Alliance is a coalition of organizations in Kansas representing school boards, teachers and teacher-educators, parents, and the Kansas Department of Education. To fulfill its mission to "make Kansas first in the nation in teaching and learning," it has developed the following rubric.

Developed by Tom Krubs, Chair, Kansas Learning First Alliance; 1420 SW Arrowhead Road, Topeka, KS 66604, www.teachkansas.org.

DRAFT   KANSAS Staff Development Rubric for District/School Assessment   DRAFT

Based on NSDC Standards

Developed by the KLFA Staff Development Sub-Committee (Revised March 26, 2002)

Standard	Level 1	Level 2	Level 3	Level 4	Evidence To Document Level
Context					
Learning Communities *Staff Development that improves the learning for all students* **organizes adults into learning communities whose goals are aligned with those of the school and the district.**	Educators seek new information, plan instruction and solve problems independently or with little collaboration with other educators. Learning and staff development is focused on individual interests and needs. Individuals make few attempts to align staff development with district or school goals for student learning.	Educators are beginning to participate in collaborative activities regarding instruction, assessment, and problem solving. Collaboration occurs infrequently and is not a regularly scheduled expectation of professional practice; the group pays minimal attention to the outcomes of student work. The work of the group is independent of district or school staff development goals.	Several of the educators have formed collaborative teams for the purpose of examining student work, planning instruction and solving problems. Educators in these teams regard team collaboration as a productive professional development activity and some teams specifically focus on improving student learning. Team planning time occurs with some regularity and school or district goals are considered as the team's work.	All educators are part of school-based learning teams that meet several times a week to plan instruction, assessment, examine student work, and/or solve problems. These teams are a primary mechanism of the school staff development plan. Team efforts align with school improvement goals and members work actively to increase student achievement.	
Leadership *Staff Development that improves the learning for all students* **requires skillful school and district leaders who guide continuous instructional improvement.**	Daily schedules and incentive systems are developed without regard to staff development. Implementation of improvement efforts typically happens independent of staff development opportunities. Training for staff development leadership is seldom provided for administrators and teacher leaders.	Daily schedules and incentive systems are designed with little consideration of ongoing professional learning. Staff development is considered necessary but seldom ties directly to goals for improvement efforts. Administrators and teacher leaders direct staff development, but with little leadership or skills training.	Yearly calendars, daily schedules, and incentive systems are designed with some connection to professional learning. Leaders acknowledge staff development as one strategy for supporting improvement. Administrators and teacher leaders occasionally share the responsibility for purposefully developing knowledge and skills for staff development leadership.	Calendars, daily schedules and incentive systems support professional learning. Leaders support staff development as a key strategy for ensuring significant improvements. Administrators and teacher leaders have opportunities to enhance their knowledge and skills to be effective staff development leaders.	

Directions: As your district/school reviews each level consider what specific evidence you have that would support the key components for that level. Level 4 contains the key elements in the NSDC Standards.   To be at Level 4, you would need clear, convincing, and consistent evidence. Evidence is measurable and furnishes proof and/or documents results. Based on this definition, what level would you rate your staff development and what evidence would you be able to provide to support your choice.

DRAFT   KANSAS Staff Development Rubric for District/School Assessment   DRAFT
Based on NSDC Standards
Developed by the KLFA Staff Development Sub-Committee (Revised March 26, 2002)

Standard	Level 1	Level 2	Level 3	Level 4	Evidence To Document Level
Resources Staff Development that improves the learning for all students *requires resources to support adult learning and collaboration.*	There is no designated budget line for staff development. There are few opportunities for staff development.	Little of the budget is set aside for staff development. Opportunities for staff development occur during the building/district scheduled in-service days.	Some of the district's budget is dedicated to staff development. Staff has worked out time for collaboration and professional learning several times a week.	The district recognizes the critical importance of professional learning and budgets accordingly.	
Process					
Data-driven Staff Development that improves the learning for all students **uses disaggregated student data to determine adult learning priorities, monitor progress, and help sustain continuous improvement.**	Staff development is planned based on individual interests of educators with little regard for student learning needs. Few attempts are made to gather school or system wide information about teacher interests. No data about student learning serve as a basis for staff development program's content.	Staff development focuses on teacher wants and interests. Surveys are focused on individual teacher needs and perceptions. Few educators collect data to determine the effects of their own learning and student progress. A few educators are reviewing student achievement data and are asking for staff development that prepares them to meet student needs more effectively.	Staff development is focused on teacher needs and based on student learning, which is monitored on a fairly regular basis. Some educators are collecting classroom-based data in order to evaluate the impact of their own learning on measures of student progress. Several staff development initiatives are created in response to this data identifying student needs.	Decisions regarding staff development are based on evidence gathered systematically in classrooms and on district and state tests. All educators routinely gather evidence of improved student learning to determine the effects of their own professional development. All staff development initiatives are based on disaggregated student data to determine adult learning priorities.	
Research-based *Staff Development that improves the learning for all students* **prepares educators to apply research to decision-making.**	Educators choose instructional strategies based on teacher preference, not on research or best practice. Staff is not knowledgeable about the action research process.	Educators are aware of the importance of selecting research-based strategies for improvement. Some staff are becoming aware of action research.	Some educators are selecting research-based strategies for improvement. Staff use pilot studies and action research to determine if programs should be adapted/continued.	Teams of educators routinely study research prior to adopting improvement strategies. Staff are skillful users of educational research and use action research to determine the impact of selected improvement strategies.	

Directions: As your district/school reviews each level consider what specific evidence you have that would support the key components for that level. Level 4 contains the key elements in the NSDC Standards. To be at Level 4, you would need clear, convincing, and consistent evidence. Evidence is measurable and furnishes proof and/or documents results. Based on this definition, what level would you rate your staff development and what evidence would you be able to provide to support your choice.

DRAFT   KANSAS Staff Development Rubric for District/School Assessment   DRAFT
Based on NSDC Standards

Developed by the KLFA Staff Development Sub-Committee (Revised March 26, 2002)

Standard	Level 1	Level 2	Level 3	Level 4	Evidence To Document Level
Evaluation *Staff Development that improves the learning for all students* **uses multiple sources of information to guide improvement and demonstrate its impact**	There are no indicators used to ensure that staff development is focused on student achievement. Evidence is not collected to determine achievement of staff development outcomes. No evidence is collected to demonstrate that implementation, follow-up strategies, and impact on student work take place.	Few indicators are used to ensure that staff development is focused on student achievement. Evidence is collected but not used to validate staff development. Evidence is collected based on immediate reactions to workshops and courses, but does not translate to student learning.	Indicators are used to guide decision-making. Some evidence is used to validate staff development. Evidence is based on initial collection of participants' reactions and begins to look at effect on student impact.	Various types of indicators are used to improve the quality of staff development. Various types of evidence are used to determine where staff development achieved its intended outcome. Evaluation of staff development includes all of the following: data concerning knowledge gained by participants, level of implementation, and changes in student learning.	
Design *Staff Development that improves the learning for all students* **through the use of learning strategies that are appropriate to the intended goal.**	Staff development opportunities are primarily limited to workshop formats. Follow-up support seldom occurs and is not a part of planning. Technology use has little if any connection to staff development designs.	Some optional staff development designs are offered in addition to workshop formats. Follow-up activities occur infrequently. Technology seldom is used as a part of staff development activities.	Several optional staff development designs are offered to support staff learning. A few designs provide opportunities for practice, feedback and implementation support. Some follow-up is available for selected innovations. Planning for technology support occasionally is a part of staff development design.	Educators regularly participate in a variety of staff development designs that facilitate staff learning, practice and implementation. Well-planned follow-up activities are incorporated in most major change initiatives. Technology is frequently integrated to support and monit or staff learning.	
Learning *Staff development that improves the learning for all students by* **applying knowledge about human learning and change**	Most staff development activities are presented without regard for differences in adult learning needs. Practice and feedback are not part of training. The change process is not considered.	Occasionally, staff development activities include opportunities for choice. Practice and feedback occur, but are not systematically incorporated. The change process receives little attention.	Learning styles, experience and skill levels are considered in the planning and delivery of staff development opportunities. Educators have some differentiated options that occasionally include practice and feedback. Some consideration of the stages in the change process is a part of planning.	Staff development options are specifically designed to accommodate and differentiate for adult learning styles, experiences and skill levels. Staff regularly experience opportunities for practice and feedback. Consideration of the adult learner's responses to the change process is systematically incorporated into staff development planning.	

Directions: As your district/school reviews each level consider what specific evidence you have that would support the key components for that level. Level 4 contains the key elements in the NSDC Standards. To be at Level 4, you would need clear, convincing, and consistent evidence. Evidence is measurable and furnishes proof and/or documents results. Based on this definition, what level would you rate your staff development and what evidence would you be able to provide to support your choice.

DRAFT   KANSAS Staff Development Rubric for District/School Assessment   DRAFT

Based on NSDC Standards

Developed by the KLFA Staff Development Sub-Committee (Revised March 26, 2002)

Standard	Level 1	Level 2	Level 3	Level 4	Evidence To Document Level
Collaboration *Staff Development that improves the learning for all students* **provides educators with the knowledge and skills to collaborate.**	Educators work in isolation and are not encouraged to collaborate. Educators who work in teams avoid controversial issues and conflict. Technology is not used by the staff as a resource.	Educators work in groups but minimal training is provided to provide staff skills in group processes. Conflict is allowed to fester or is avoided and is not resolved. Technology is not seen as a tool for collaboration purposes.	Staff development is provided to prepare staff to work collaboratively Conflict is talked about and is often resolved. Technology is used in some situations as a resource for collaboration.	Educators have the structures and training to be skillful members of a variety of groups. Educators have and use skills to surface and productively manage conflict and reach consensus decisions. Educators know how to use technology for different forms of collaboration.	
Content					
Equity *Staff Development that improves the learning for all students* **prepares educators to understand and appreciate all students, create safe, orderly, and supportive learning environments, and hold high expectations for students' academic achievement.**	Educators use teacher-centered curriculum and instruction with minimal awareness of the cultural backgrounds of their students. Educators continue to implement the same lesson plans year after year. Student expectations are not established.	Learning related to culture and diversity encourages educators to plan cultural activities around holidays. Staff are provided training on individualizing instruction but the achievement gap is not closing. Staff development is focused on helping educators remediate students.	Some educators implement practices that promote safe environments and convey respect for all students, their families and students' diverse backgrounds. Educators are provided training to help them to individualize instruction to close the achievement gap but are inconsistently applying what they have learned. Staff knows the importance of high expectations.	Educators implement school-wide practices that promote safe environments and convey respect for all students, their families and students' diverse backgrounds. Educators are closing the achievement gap by adjusting instruction and assessment to match the learning requirements of individual students. Staff establish learning environments that communicate high expectations for all students.	

Directions: As your district/school reviews each level consider what specific evidence you have that would support the key components for that level. Level 4 contains the key elements in the NSDC Standards. To be at Level 4, you would need clear, convincing, and consistent evidence. Evidence is measurable and furnishes proof and/or documents results. Based on this definition, what level would you rate your staff development and what evidence would you be able to provide to support your choice.

DRAFT KANSAS Staff Development Rubric for District/School Assessment DRAFT
Based on NSDC Standards
Developed by the KLFA Staff Development Sub-Committee (Revised March 26, 2002)

Standard	Level 1	Level 2	Level 3	Level 4	Evidence To Document Level
Quality Teaching *Staff Development that improves the learning for all students* **deepens educators' content knowledge, provides them with research-based instructional strategies to assist students in meeting rigorous academic standards, and prepares them to use various types of classroom assessments appropriately.**	Staff development opportunities occur sporadically without regard to needs for developing deeper content knowledge. Instruction is focused on covering the curriculum Classroom assessment is used to support grades for progress reporting.	Opportunities are offered for educators to increase content knowledge but most are associated with implementation of new curriculum. Occasional staff development for instructional skills occurs but is independent of improvement plans and content area. Staff development efforts occasionally provide educators with knowledge of some classroom assessment strategies.	Staff has opportunities to develop knowledge of their content area. Several opportunities are available to learn and practice instructional skills but most are independent of content areas. Some staff development is available regarding classroom assessment methods and some educators are beginning to regularly use assessment strategies to monitor gains in student learning.	Staff have many opportunities to develop deep knowledge of their content. Staff development expands instructional methods appropriate to specific content areas. Educators learn and implement classroom assessment skills that allow them to regularly monitor gains in student learning.	
Family Involvement: *Staff Development that improves the learning for all students* **provides educators with knowledge and skills to involve families and other stakeholders appropriately.**	Staff have no strategies in place to ask for and/or implement input from community members and parents. Parent participation is thought of as intrusive and unwanted. There is no technology available for enhancing communication with the community.	Staff use groups like site councils, to seek input from the community and parents, but little if any of the suggestions are implemented. The goals and mission continue to be developed by the school staff. Educators communicate with parents by phone and to some degree through e-mails.	Staff recognizes the need for training and technical assistance in how to build consensus among educators and community members concerning the overall mission and goals for staff development. Educators create relationships with parents to support student learning. Training in the use of technology to communicate with parents and the community is improving as staff acquire better skill in the use of technology.	Staff development prepares administrators and teacher leaders to build consensus among educators and community members concerning the overall mission and goals for staff development. Educators establish relationships with parents to support student learning. Technology is used to communicate with parents and the community.	

Directions: As your district/school reviews each level consider what specific evidence you have that would support the key components for that level. Level 4 contains the key elements in the NSDC Standards. To be at Level 4, you would need clear, convincing, and consistent evidence. Evidence is measurable and furnishes proof and/or documents results. Based on this definition, what level would you rate your staff development and what evidence would you be able to provide to support your choice.

How To Plan
for Successful Staff Development

Administrator   All Grade Levels   Professional Development
Teacher

Most staff development activities do not work, for a variety of reasons. The most common reason is that bridges have not been built to connect workshops to the needs of the staff. Sally Zepeda, in her book *The Principal as Instructional Leader,* questions that principals and school leadership teams need to answer to make professional development more successful.

- What staff development is needed at the school?
- What planning for staff development needs to be completed?
- What resources (physical, financial, and human) are needed to provide staff development?
- What follow-up activities are needed to support the application and extension of skills learned during staff development?
- How can the overall impact of staff development on student and teacher learning be evaluated?
- Who will conduct staff development?
- Does staff development align with site-level goals?

Checklist
for Running Good Staff Meetings

Administrator   **All Grade Levels**   **Professional Development**
Teacher

Staff meetings are a necessary evil. They must be held, and sometimes the faculty objects to attending them. Frequently—too frequently—they deal with trivial or administrative items. Sometimes they fail to address issues of learning and teaching. The following checklist is offered to help turn staff meetings into productive meetings.

- ◆ **Schedule meetings in advance.** Give your faculty enough advance notice so that they can clear their calendars and prepare material if necessary. If possible, set a regular meeting time and place. Let the staff know the schedule in advance.

- ◆ **Actively encourage attendance.** Make it a point to convey the importance of attending. Try to get everyone to attend (counselors, psychologists, social workers, attendance teachers, and all other support staff). If the head of the parents' association can attend, invite him or her if the agenda has anything to do with parents.

- ◆ **Distribute an agenda in advance.** Give a paragraph summary of the items to be discussed. Agendas orient attendees and save time.

- ◆ **Move swiftly from topic to topic.** Give sufficient time to discuss each item, but move the agenda forward so that the meeting does not degenerate into a gripe session.

- ◆ **Be receptive to questions, concerns, and suggestions.** Keep the tone positive, but do not steer discussions away from difficult topics that deserve a hearing.

- ◆ **Make time for follow-up.** Arrange for follow-up meetings with individuals whose needs are too specific or too complex to be met at a general staff meeting.

- ◆ **Serve refreshments.** See whether a business partner, the school cafeteria, or a local fast-food place can supply refreshments at little or no cost. This makes the meeting a more social event.

- ◆ **Have minutes taken.** Follow up on agenda items that were discussed but need additional time or actions. Discuss these items with staff at the next scheduled meeting.

Active Learning

Active learning embraces teaching and learning strategies that engage and involve students in the learning process. Students find new and creative ways to solve problems, achieve success, and become lifelong learners when educators show them there are different ways to learn. The following tools are included in this chapter:

Teaching At-Risk Students with ADD and ADHD, developed by Cindy Jones, Education Support Associates, Inc.; 4246 Fossil Lane, San Antonio, TX 78261, www.educationsupportassociates.com, cindypurcelljones@earthlink.net.

How Do Different Children Learn in Different Ways? developed by Cindy Jones, Education Support Associates, Inc.; 4246 Fossil Lane, San Antonio, TX 78261, www.educationsupportassociates.com, cindypurcelljones@earthlink.net.

It's Not How Smart You Are—It's How You Are Smart, developed and written by Walter McKenzie, Consultant, Surfaquarium; 18 Olde Taverne Lane, Amesbury, MA 01913, www.surfaquarium.com.

Multiple Intelligences Inventory, developed and written by Walter McKenzie, Consultant, Surfaquarium; 18 Olde Taverne Lane, Amesbury, MA 01913, www. surfaquarium.com.

Teaching At-Risk Students with ADD and ADHD

Special Educator   Middle School   Active Learning
Teacher   High School   Alternative Schooling
                                                    Individualized Instruction

Many of our at-risk students are special education students. Cindy Jones of Education Support Associates Inc. has done intensive study of current brain research on learning-disabled students and has granted permission to share it with our readers.

Strategies

- Provide two desks 10 feet apart. Allow the student to work at each desk. The student can move between the two desks as long as he or she does not bother others during the transition.
- Attach a bungee cord to the legs of the desk. Allow the student to bounce his or her feet.
- Allow student to walk around doing his or her work on a clipboard.
- Allow student to use a standing desk (such as the top of a bookcase.)
- Allow student to tap with a straw or squeeze a stress ball.
- Use desk templates for organization of materials. Allow time at the end of each day for organization.
- Assign a study buddy.
- Have a daily schedule and stick to it.
- Alternate between active and quiet activities.
- Allow frequent brain breaks.
- Limit down time.
- Help students organize long-term projects.
- Use team and learning partners.
- Use contracts and reinforcement systems.
- Use a three-minute warning system.
- Teach desired procedures.

How Do Different Children Learn in Different Ways?

Administrator	Middle School	Active Learning
Special Educator	High School	Alternative Schooling
Teacher		Individualized Instruction

We now know enough about brain research to know that children learn in different ways and at different paces. We also know something about what inhibits their learning. Cindy Jones of Education Support Associates Inc. has done intensive study of current brain research and has granted permission to share it with our readers.

♦ Many at-risk students are actually in survival mode. Their threatening home and school environments cause the brain chemical *serotonin* to be reduced. Serotonin is a strong regulator of emotion. When its levels are reduced, students may become outwardly aggressive (with physical or verbal actions) or inwardly aggressive (with depression).

♦ Threats and stress tend to elevate the brain chemical *vasopressin*. When this chemical is elevated, it can lead to aggressive behavior. An imbalance in either of these chemicals can lead to a lifetime of violent behavior. Some of the behaviors that may result from these imbalances include

  • Creating a chaotic environment around themselves because it feels normal

  • Swatting or threatening others to establish rank in the classroom

  • Making statements such as "he's looking at me!" to guard one's territory

  • Misreading gestures and facial expressions and thinking that every one represents anger

♦ Many students misbehave in class because they are bored and their minds begin to wander. After 17 minutes of sitting, blood begins to pool in the hamstrings and *melatonin* is released. This causes a state of sleepiness. Have students stand and move or exercise at their desks. This causes blood to go to the brain, thereby increasing attention arousal and speeding up information processing.

♦ To keep students focused, it is important to change the learner's state *every 7–10 minutes*. This means that you stop doing what you are doing and do something different. For example, when you see a student's face glaze over, change your voice, play a short blast of rock-and-roll music, tell the class to stand up and discuss a point, or pull out an unusual prop.

♦ *Sifting* is also an important concept for the student's retention of new learning. Sifting means that you stop and ask students to make the learning personal. This should be done *every 20–30 minutes*. The student could talk with a partner about what he or she has learned or draw a picture or diagram of the learning. The whole class could make a mind map together. This process will ensure that the new learning goes into short-term memory, where it can be assimilated into long-term memory while the student is sleeping.

♦ Brains have been rewired during the last 20 years. The excessive use of television, video games, and movies has caused the percentage of students who are visual and kinesthetic learners to increase greatly. Most special education students are not auditory learners. Therefore, the lecture model does not work well for them.

♦ Rituals create a sense of safety. The brain craves two things, *novelty* and *ritual.*

  • Novelty is what keeps students focused on the instruction. Novelty strategies might include the use of a prop, story, or activity.

  • Ritual means that procedures are the same every day. These help students to feel a sense of safety in the classroom.

♦ The following characteristics are common among learning-disabled students:

  • Disorganized and frustrated in new learning situations

  • Overwhelmed in new situations or when new content is presented

  • Difficulty structuring work time

  • Trouble following instructions

  • Easily distracted

  • Poor social judgment

  • Lack of connection between effort and success

  • Trouble with paper-and-pencil tasks

  • Low level of frustration

It's Not How Smart You Are— It's How You Are Smart

Teacher	All Grade Levels	Active Learning
Administrator		Alternative Schooling
Special Educator		Individualized Instruction
Counselor		

Walter McKenzie has written a clear description of Howard Gardner's concept of "multiple intelligences."

Howard Gardner's Theory of Multiple Intelligences

What parent cannot see gleaming rays of genius in his or her child? And yet, how many children come to school and demonstrate their own unique genius? There was a time when it might have been a joke to suggest that "every parent thinks their kid's a genius." But current research on human intelligence suggests the joke may be on educators. There is a constant flow of new information on how the human brain operates, how it differs in function between genders, how emotions effect intellectual acuity, even how genetics and environment each affect our children's cognitive abilities. Although each area of study has its merits, Howard Gardner of Harvard University has identified different kinds of intelligence that we possess. This has particularly strong ramifications in the classroom: If we can identify children's different strengths among these intelligences, we can accommodate different children more successfully according to their orientation to learning.

Thus far, Gardner's work suggests nine intelligences. He speculates there may be many more that have not yet been identified. Time will tell. These are the paths to children's learning that teachers can address in their classrooms right now. The nine intelligences are the following:

1. Visual/spatial—children who learn best visually and organize things spatially. They like to see what you are talking about in order to understand. They enjoy charts, graphs, maps, tables, illustrations, art, puzzles, and costumes—anything eye catching.

2. Verbal/linguistic—children who demonstrate strength in the language arts: speaking, writing, reading, and listening. These students have always been successful in traditional classrooms because their intelligence lends itself to traditional teaching.

3. Mathematical/logical—children who display an aptitude for numbers, reasoning, and problem solving. These children have also typically done well in traditional classrooms, where teaching is logically sequenced and students are asked to conform.

4. Bodily/kinesthetic—children who experience learning best through activity: games, movement, hands-on tasks, and building. These children often have been labeled "overly active" in traditional classrooms, where they are told to sit and be still!

5. Musical/rhythmic—children who learn well through songs, patterns, rhythms, instruments, and musical expression. It is easy to overlook children with this intelligence in traditional education.

6. Intrapersonal—children who are especially in touch with their own feelings, values, and ideas. They may tend to be more reserved, but they are actually quite intuitive about what they learn and how it relates to themselves.

7. Interpersonal—children who are noticeably people oriented and outgoing and do their learning cooperatively in groups or with a partner. These children typically have been identified as "talkative" or "too concerned about being social" in traditional settings.

8. Naturalist—children who love the outdoors, animals, and field trips. More than this, though, these students love to pick up on subtle differences in meanings. The traditional classroom has not been accommodating to these children.

9. Existentialist—children who learn in the context of humankind's place in the "big picture" of existence. They ask "why are we here?" and "what is our role in the world?" This intelligence is seen in the discipline of philosophy.

Teachers are now working on assimilating this knowledge into their strategies for helping children learn. Although it is too early to know the ramifications of this research, it is clear that the day has past when educators could teach the textbook, and it is the dawn of educators teaching each child according to his or her orientation to the world.

Multiple Intelligences Inventory

Counselor   All Grade Levels   Active Learning
Teacher   Alternative Schooling
Individualized Instruction

Walter McKenzie developed a system of measuring multiple intelligences. This is not a test—it is a snapshot in time of an individual's perceived multiple intelligences preferences.

Are you looking for a picture-based inventory for nonreaders or an Excel-based inventory that automatically completes your multiple intelligences profile for you? Walter's first book offers both on CD-ROM.

Part I

Complete each section by placing a "1" next to each statement you feel accurately describes you. If you do not identify with a statement, leave the space blank. Then total the columns in each section.

Section 1

_____ I enjoy categorizing things by common traits.
_____ Ecological issues are important to me.
_____ Hiking and camping are enjoyable activities.
_____ I enjoy working in a garden.
_____ I believe preserving our national parks is important.
_____ Putting things in hierarchies makes sense to me.
_____ Animals are important in my life.
_____ My home has a recycling system in place.
_____ I enjoy studying biology, botany, and/or zoology.
_____ I spend a great deal of time outdoors.
_____ **Total for Section 1**

Section 2

_____ I easily pick up on patterns.
_____ I focus on noise and sounds.
_____ Moving to a beat is easy for me.
_____ I've always been interested in playing an instrument.
_____ The cadence of poetry intrigues me.
_____ I remember things by putting them in a rhyme.
_____ Concentration is difficult while listening to a radio or television.
_____ I enjoy many kinds of music.
_____ Musicals are more interesting than dramatic plays.
_____ Remembering song lyrics is easy for me.
_____ **Total for Section 2**

Section 3

_____ I keep my things neat and orderly.

_____ Step-by-step directions are a big help.

_____ Solving problems comes easily to me.

_____ I get easily frustrated with disorganized people.

_____ I can complete calculations quickly in my head.

_____ Puzzles requiring reasoning are fun.

_____ I can't begin an assignment until all my questions are answered.

_____ Structure helps me to be successful.

_____ I find working on a computer spreadsheet or database rewarding.

_____ Things have to make sense to me or I am dissatisfied.

_____ **Total for Section 3**

Section 4

_____ It is important to see my role in the "big picture" of things.

_____ I enjoy discussing questions about life.

_____ Religion is important to me.

_____ I enjoy viewing art masterpieces.

_____ Relaxation and meditation exercises are rewarding.

_____ I like visiting breathtaking sites in nature.

_____ I enjoy reading ancient and modern philosophers.

_____ Learning new things is easier when I understand their value.

_____ I wonder whether there are other forms of intelligent life in the universe.

_____ Studying history and ancient culture helps give me perspective.

_____ **Total for Section 4**

Section 5

_____ I learn best by interacting with others.

_____ I believe the more, the merrier.

_____ Study groups are very productive for me.

_____ I enjoy chat rooms.

_____ Participating in politics is important.

_____ Television and radio talk shows are enjoyable.

_____ I am a "team player."

_____ I dislike working alone.

_____ Clubs and extracurricular activities are fun.

_____ I pay attention to social issues and causes.

_____ **Total for Section 5**

Section 6

_____ I enjoy making things with my hands.
_____ Sitting still for long periods of time is difficult for me.
_____ I enjoy outdoor games and sports.
_____ I value nonverbal communication such as sign language.
_____ A fit body is important for a fit mind.
_____ Arts and crafts are enjoyable pastimes.
_____ Expression through dance is beautiful.
_____ I like working with tools.
_____ I live an active lifestyle.
_____ I learn by doing.
_____ **Total for Section 6**

Section 7

_____ I enjoy reading all kinds of materials.
_____ Taking notes helps me remember and understand.
_____ I faithfully contact friends through letters and/or e-mail.
_____ It is easy for me to explain my ideas to others.
_____ I keep a journal.
_____ Word puzzles such as crosswords and jumbles are fun.
_____ I write for pleasure.
_____ I enjoy playing with words like puns, anagrams, and spoonerisms.
_____ Foreign languages interest me.
_____ Debates and public speaking are activities I like to participate in.
_____ **Total for Section 7**

Section 8

_____ I am keenly aware of my moral beliefs.
_____ I learn best when I have an emotional attachment to the subject.
_____ Fairness is important to me.
_____ My attitude affects how I learn.
_____ Social justice issues concern me.
_____ Working alone can be just as productive as working in a group.
_____ I need to know why I should do something before I agree to do it.
_____ When I believe in something, I will give 100% of my effort to it.
_____ I like to be involved in causes that help others.
_____ I am willing to protest or sign a petition to right a wrong.
_____ **Total for Section 8**

Section 9

_____ I can imagine ideas in my mind.
_____ Rearranging a room is fun for me.
_____ I enjoy creating art using varied media.
_____ I remember well using graphic organizers.
_____ Performance art can be very gratifying.
_____ Spreadsheets are great for making charts, graphs, and tables.
_____ Three-dimensional puzzles bring me much enjoyment.
_____ Music videos are very stimulating.
_____ I can recall things in mental pictures.
_____ I am good at reading maps and blueprints.
_____ **Total for Section 9**

Part II

Carry forward your totals from each section and multiply each by 10:

Section	Total Forward	Multiply	Score
1		x 10	
2		x 10	
3		x 10	
4		x 10	
5		x 10	
6		x 10	
7		x 10	
8		x 10	
9		x 10	

Part III

Plot your scores on the bar graph provided:

	Sec 1	Sec 2	Sec 3	Sec 4	Sec 5	Sec 6	Sec 7	Sec 8	Sec 9
100									
90									
80									
70									
60									
50									
40									
30									
20									
10									
0									

Part IV

Key:

Section 1 reflects your *naturalist* strength.

Section 2 suggests your *musical* strength.

Section 3 indicates your *logical* strength.

Section 4 illustrates your *existential* strength.

Section 5 shows your *interpersonal* strength.

Section 6 tells your *kinesthetic* strength.

Section 7 indicates your *verbal* strength.

Section 8 reflects your intrapersonal *strength.*

Section 9 suggests your *visual* strength.

Remember:

♦ Everyone has all of the intelligences.

♦ You can strengthen an intelligence.

♦ This inventory is meant as a snapshot in time—it can change.

♦ Multiple intelligences is meant to empower, not label people.

Educational Technology

Technology offers some of the best opportunities for delivering instruction to engage students in authentic learning, addressing multiple intelligences, and adapting to students' learning styles. The following tools are included in this chapter:

What Benchmarks Can Schools Use to Indicate Progress? excerpted from *An Educator's Guide to Evaluating the Use of Technology in Schools and Classrooms*, U.S. Department of Education, Office of Educational Research and Improvement, 1998.

Using Technology to Make Connections Between School and Family, developed by Franklin P. Schargel.

What Indicators Can Schools Use to Show Progress? excerpted from *An Educator's Guide to Evaluating the Use of Technology in Schools and Classrooms*, U.S. Department of Education, Office of Educational Research and Improvement, 1998.

What Benchmarks Can Schools Use
to Indicate Progress?

Administrator   All Grade Levels   After-School Opportunities
Counselor   Educational Technology
Special Educator   Professional Development
Teacher   School–Community Collaboration

Benchmarks provide a sense of what the program is striving to attain, either on an incremental basis (e.g., every two years test scores will rise 2 percentage points) or as a final target (e.g., all students will score at or above the proficiency level). Two important factors need to be considered when setting benchmarks: the resources available to the program and a starting point or baseline. For example, if you were evaluating a relatively small initiative that is funding the purchase of new equipment, you would not expect the student-to-computer ratio to increase to the same extent as it would in a program that provides more extensive funding. Baselines are also important because they help to establish the amount of change one can realistically expect. Let's assume that the purpose of the program you are evaluating is to improve student reading. To set an appropriate benchmark, you would need to determine student performance before the program began. This is considered a baseline, a point from which to measure change and to determine appropriate benchmarks.

Indicator	Benchmark
Increasing numbers of teachers will be trained to integrate technology into their teaching.	By the end of the school year, 50% of teachers will have had technology training.
Teachers will learn how to integrate technology into their teaching.	After training, teachers will be able to devise at least three examples of how technology could be integrated into their lessons.
Teacher-to-computer and student-to-computer ratios will steadily decline.	By next year, teacher-to-computer and student-to-computer ratios schoolwide (counting all computers) will be 4:1 and 6:1.
Students will actively use computers for projects and assignments.	All students will use computers at school at least four hours per week.
Technology will be increasingly incorporated into the curriculum in all subject areas.	In two years, English, science, and social studies curricula will have a least 25 percent of lessons incorporating technology.
An increasing percentage of teacher lessons will incorporate technology.	All trained teachers will have at least 25 percent of lessons incorporating technology.
Outcome	**Benchmark**
Students will produce reports and presentations that teachers judge to be of higher quality.	Within two years, student grades will increase, on average, by 10 points or one letter grade. (Figures used are examples only; the actual percentages may vary.)
Students will display increasingly higher performance on tests assessing reading ability.	Within two years, student scores on the reading portion of standardized tests will increase by 10 percent.
Both teachers and students will display increased computer literacy.	After one year, at least 75 percent of teachers and students will display at least an intermediate level of computer literacy.

Using Technology to Make Connections between School and Family

Administrator   All Grade Levels   Educational Technology
Teacher   Family Engagement
Counselor   Professional Development
                                                        School–Community Collaboration

How can schools use technology to communicate with families more frequently and efficiently? To help families support students' learning at home? Or to receive input from families and community members about school issues and district policies?

Technology provides an additional resource that allows a two-way dialogue between home and school, between teacher and home, and between teacher and student.

- Welcome new families and students to the school.
- Create a lending library of books, videos, and audiotapes to aid parents in helping their children to read and do homework and to learn about child development.
- Use the school's automated phone system to alert families about report card distribution, early dismissals, and school events such as plays or sporting events.
- Create a homework help line that allows students and their parents to get information on and assistance with homework.
- Provide absent students and their parents a way to receive work missed.
- During nonschool hours, invite families and community members to use school computers to learn skills such as keyboarding and software applications.
- Have the school serve as a resource to enable parents and students to purchase computer hardware and software through the school's mass-purchasing ability.
- Have teachers use e-mail to share information with students and their families about homework policies, lateness and absence directives, the student's performance, curriculum-related television programs, and useful Web sites.
- Allow parents to e-mail teachers with questions, suggestions, and comments.
- Have principals e-mail families about parent organization meetings, school board meetings, general election information, and electronic versions of newsletters.

- Over a secure, password-protected line, allow families to get student grades and report cards.
- Give students extra assignments and enriched curriculum.
- Have counselors direct students to college and university Web sites and career and technical education information.
- Have computer-knowledgeable parents assist the school in making purchases of software and hardware by serving on the school's technology committee.

What Indicators Can
Schools Use to Show Progress?

Administrator   All Grade Levels   After-School Opportunities
Teacher   Educational Technology
                                                         Professional Development
                                                School–Community Collaboration

Evaluating educational technology programs can be a challenging endeavor. Having developed goals, schools also must develop indicators. Indicators are statements that reflect specific goals than can be used to gauge progress. Indicators help to orient you toward a measure of performance outcomes and typically focus on only one aspect of a goal.

Goal	Indicators
Professional development	Increasing numbers of teachers will be trained to integrate technology into their teaching. Teachers will learn how to integrate technology into their teaching.
Availability of technology	Teacher-to-computer and student-to-computer ratios will decline steadily. Students will actively use computers for projects and assignments.
Curriculum integration	Technology will be increasingly incorporated into the curriculum in all subject areas. An increasing percentage of teacher lessons will incorporate technology.
Outcome	*Indicators*
Reading and writing	Students will produce reports and presentations that teachers judge to be of higher quality. Students will display increasingly higher performance on tests assessing reading ability.
Computer literacy	Both teachers and student will display increased computer literacy.

Good indicators should do the following:

♦ **Include relevant measures**—Indicators should be designed with thought toward the information that could be collected to inform them.

♦ **Address appropriate groups**—Indicators should consider any subpopulations that need to be examined separately (such as school level, racial or ethnic group, or special education).

♦ **Be few**—You do not need a lot of indicators to convey a lot of information.

- **Be actionable**—Indicators should guide improvement by identifying programs that are working and those that are not, by helping administrators to make decisions to improve results, and by helping policy makers to judge progress toward goals.
- **Be timely**—Indicators should be as useful next year as they are today.
- **Be reliable**—Indicators should be easily measured by a variety of people and across time.
- **Be comparable**—Measures developed from the present indicators should be able to be comparable to measures developed from similar indicators in the past.

Individualized Instruction

Each student has unique interests and past learning experiences. An individualized instructional program for each student allows for flexibility in teaching methods and motivational strategies that consider these individual differences. The following tools are included in this chapter:

Individualized Learning Plan, developed by Franklin P. Schargel.

Intake Interview Form, developed by Franklin P. Schargel.

Reducing Special Education Dropouts by Meeting Individual Student Needs, adapted from J.A. Pauley. D.F. Bradley and J.F. Pauley, *Here's How to Reach Me: Matching Instruction to Personality Types in Your Classroom* (Paul H. Brookes Publishing Co., 2002); T. Kahler, *Personality Pattern Inventory Validation Studies* (Kahler Communications, 1982); and T. Kahler, *Personality Pattern Inventory* (Kahler Communications, 1996). Adapted by Judith Ann Pauley, Adjunct Professor, California State University, San Marcos, and Joseph F. Pauley, Adjunct Professor, McDaniel College, Maryland. Permission given by authors and publishers.

How to Reduce the At-Risk Population by Meeting Individual Needs, adapted from J.A. Pauley. D.F. Bradley and J.F. Pauley, *Here's How to Reach Me: Matching Instruction to Personality Types in Your Classroom* (Paul H. Brookes Publishing Co., 2002); T. Kahler, *Personality Pattern Inventory Validation Studies* (Kahler Communications, 1982); and T. Kahler, *Personality Pattern Inventory* (Kahler Communications, 1996). Adapted by Judith Ann Pauley, Adjunct Professor, California State University, San Marcos, and Joseph F. Pauley, Adjunct Professor, McDaniel College, Maryland. Permission given by authors and publishers.

Individualized Learning Plan

Administrator	Middle School	Alternative Schooling
Counselor	High School	Individualized Instruction
Teacher		Professional Development

Individualized learning plans can aid at-risk students by specifying what the student will learn and how that learning will take place. Most educators are unfamiliar with what a learning plan is.

What Is a Learning Plan?

A learning plan is a document developed by a student and his or her teacher that specifies what the student will learn and how the learning will take place during a given period of time. It describes the structure of the learning experience with respect to individual goals and objectives.

Types of Plans

There are two types of individualized learning plans. The first kind of plan is a *working plan.* It specifies specific time commitments, physical arrangements and requirements, and roles and responsibilities. The second type is a *learning plan.* This plan consists of three parts: (1) learning objectives, (2) learning activities, and (3) strategies and methods of evaluation.

Why Use a Learning Plan?

♦ It specifies a purpose, target issues, and clearly defined goals and objectives.
♦ It defines expectations.
♦ It enables students to participate more actively in the evaluation of their own learning.
♦ It lays out an explicit road map of what the student needs to work toward.

Why Set Goals?

♦ They involve the student and the teacher in providing direction for the learning process.
♦ They provide criteria against which to measure progress and performance.

Questions to Help Develop the Learning Plan

The following questions may be useful as the student and educator work together to develop a learning plan:

♦ What are our expectations of each other?
♦ Are our goals the same?
♦ Can we achieve them?
♦ How can we achieve them?
♦ What constraints exist?
♦ How will we know when we have achieved the goals?

Setting Goals

The goals of the learning plan should have the following characteristics:

♦ Specific
♦ Achievable over time
♦ Measurable
♦ Realistic
♦ Related to the task formulated
♦ Modifiable over time
♦ Seen in light of constraints
♦ Ordered in priority

Intake Interview Form

Administrator   Middle School   Alternative Schooling
Counselor   High School   Individualized Instruction
Teacher   Mentoring and Tutoring
                                                          Safe Learning Environments

Many at-risk students transfer from one public school to another, from one public school to a charter or private school, or from a school to a recovery program. This intake interview form provides the counselor with vital information and can be used to open a dialogue.

Please check the reason(s) why you did not attend school on a regular basis. (You may check more than one.)

☐ You did not like school.

☐ You did not feel safe in school.

☐ You had poor grades.

☐ You were working, offered a job, or decided to seek employment.

☐ You could not get along with teachers or other school personnel.

☐ You could not get along with other students.

☐ You had to support your family.

☐ You had other responsibilities at home.

☐ You were pregnant, got married, or became a parent.

☐ You were expelled or suspended.

☐ You had a drug and/or alcohol problem.

☐ You were arrested or involved with the legal system.

☐ You needed to work.

☐ You were picked on by other students (bullied).

☐ Your family moved.

☐ Your neighborhood was dangerous.

☐ Other (explain):

Reducing Special Education Dropouts by Meeting Individual Student Needs

Special Educator
Teacher

All Grade Levels

Active Learning
Individualized Instruction
Professional Development

Many students who have problems in school and decide to drop out at a very early age are very intelligent people. Why do they drop out, and how can teachers reach and teach them? Recent research shows that many dropouts have one of two personality types. Many are creative, spontaneous, and playful or they are resourceful, adaptable, and charming. Both types tend to be kinesthetic learners who need action, fun, or excitement in their classwork to have energy to do their work. If teachers do not include something in each lesson that motivates these two personality types, the students will do something negative to create the fun or excitement. The creative students may act out or become the class clown, and the resourceful ones may manipulate, con, or make fools of others. Both will break class rules. Research shows these negative behaviors will stop or be greatly reduced if teachers include something fun or exciting in each class.

Below is a partial list of things that teachers can do to motivate these two types of students.

- Help them memorize by setting lessons to music
- Allow them to stand periodically
- Have them move from place to place
- Have them share in groups
- Have them share in pairs
- Have them present in front of the class
- Create a casual atmosphere
- Permit casual dress
- Give friendly greetings (high fives)
- Use overheads and other visual aids
- Play loud background music periodically during a lesson
- Allow them to stand near their desks periodically
- Have them write lists on blackboard as class scribes
- Use colorful posters

- Have them vote for what they like or don't like
- Involve them in decision making
- Let them create a song or poem and read it to the class
- Have them act out parts in plays or stories
- Use team competitions within the class and give rewards to the winning team
- Award prizes for academic excellence
- Give quick rewards
- Speak their language
- Tie the lesson to the big picture and show how they can use it in real life
- Set short-term interim goals for resourceful students with rewards along the way
- Make deals with them

- Use videos to illustrate points or stimulate discussion
- Allow them to move in place periodically
- Encourage them to participate actively in demonstrations
- Write in colors, especially in blue and red
- Use colorful overheads and graphs
- Use humor (not sarcasm) in your classes
- Use visual cartoons
- Encourage them to learn through role playing
- Use games to teach lessons
- Make demonstrations fun
- Have them share while standing
- Have them share while sitting
- Let them stand when answering questions
- Give advance notice when ending discussion sessions
- Create a lively environment
- Be creative in planning lessons
- Make presentations energetic
- Speak in a fun, lighthearted manner with creative students

- Give resourceful students a chance to look good in front of their peers
- Provide opportunities for positive competition in the classroom
- Be direct in ordering resourceful students to do things
- Use redeemable chits as rewards for scholarship
- Let them be peer tutors
- Let them sing songs (you lead or they lead)
- Let them draw pictures
- Change strategies frequently
- Do the unexpected from time to time within a structured framework
- Let them work as a team
- Encourage cooperative learning
- Vary the pace of the class
- Use in-school and out-of-school field trips
- Allow them to be creative in doing their homework
- Give resourceful students a chance to be a leader in class
- Channel student energy positively
- Send students on errands
- Allow creative students to do their classwork on the floor near their seats

Adapted by permission from Pauley, J.A., Bradley, D.F., & Pauley, J.F. (2002). *Here's How to Reach Me: Matching Instruction to Personality Types in Your Classroom* (p. 83). Baltimore: Paul H. Brookes Publishing Co. www.brookespublishing.com

How To Reduce the At-Risk Population by Meeting Individual Needs

Special Educator Teacher	All Grade Levels	Individualized Instruction Professional Development

Many students who have problems in school and decide to drop out at a very early age are very intelligent people. Why do they drop out, and how can teachers reach and teach them? Recent research shows that many dropouts have one of two personality types. Many are creative, spontaneous, and playful or they are resourceful, adaptable, and charming. Both types tend to be kinesthetic learners who need action, fun, or excitement in their classwork to have energy to do their work. If teachers do not include something in each lesson that motivates these two personality types, the students will do something negative to create the fun or excitement. The creative students may act out or become the class clown, and the resourceful ones may manipulate, con, or make fools of others. Both will break class rules. Research shows these negative behaviors will stop or be greatly reduced if teachers include something fun or exciting in each class.

The following is a partial list of things that teachers can do to motivate these two types of students.

Play loud music
Stand periodically
Move from place to place
Share in groups
Share in pairs
Present in front of the class
Create a casual atmosphere
Allow casual dress
Give friendly greetings (high fives)
Use visual aids (overheads)
Play loud background music
Think on their feet
Have them write lists

Play games
Use fun demonstrations
Share while standing
Share while sitting
Answer questions
Give advance notice when ending discussion sessions
Use colorful graphs
Create a lively environment
Give an energetic presentation
Speak in a fun, lighthearted manner with creative students
Involve them in decisionmaking

Give prizes
Have math teams competing with another team
Give quick rewards
Speak their language
Tie lessons to the big picture and real life
Set short-term interim goals for resourceful students with rewards along the way
Make deals
Give resourceful students a chance to look good in front of their peers
Provide opportunities for positive competition in the classroom

Use colorful posters

Play videos

Move in place

Actively participate in demonstrations

Write in blue and red

Use colorful overheads

Use humor

Use visual cartoons

Role playing

Do the unexpected from time to time within a structured framework

Work as a team

Learn cooperatively

Vary the pace of the class

Be direct in ordering resourceful students to do things

Have students vote for what they like or don't like

Let students create a song or poem and read it to class

Have students act out a part in a play or story

Arrange in-school and out-of-school field trips

Allow them to be creative in doing their homework

Give resourceful students a chance to be a leader in class

Give redeemable chits as rewards for scholarship

Provide peer tutors

Let them sing songs (you lead or they lead)

Let them draw pictures

Change strategies frequently

Channel student energy positively

Send students on errands

Allow creative students to do their classwork on the floor near their seats

Adapted by permission from Pauley, J.A., Bradley, D.F., & Pauley, J.F. (2002). *Here's How to Reach Me: Matching Instruction to Personality Types in Your Classroom* (p. 96). Baltimore: Paul H. Brookes Publishing Co. www.brookespublishing.com

Career and Technical Education

A quality career and technical education (CTE) program and a related guidance program are essential for all students. School-to-work programs recognize that youth need specific skills to prepare them to measure up to the larger demands of today's workplace. The following tools are included in this chapter:

How to Create Successful School-to-Work Projects, developed by Arnold H. Packer. In his book *School-to-Work* (coauthored with Marion W. Pines, M. Frank Stluka, and Christine Surowiec; Eye on Education, 1996), Packer identified seven essential elements of the school-to-work projects he investigated in his research. Used with the permission of the publisher.

How to Develop an Individualized Career and Educational Plan. This document is based on career and educational planning components prescribed by the National Council of Research in Vocational Education at the University of California, Berkeley, Office of Student Services, and the work of Dennis Dilton at Rock Island High School.

How To Create Successful School-to-Work Projects

Administrator   Middle School   Alternative Schooling
Teacher   High School   Career and Technical Education
                                              School–Community Collaboration
                                              Service Learning

Cooperation among Teachers

Most school-to-work projects are the product of two or more teachers working together. Students can then work on their projects during more than one class period per day. This also expands the knowledge base from which the teachers draw, allowing them to show students how lessons from at least two academic disciplines apply to their work.

Resourcefulness

Teachers must take stock of the resources available to them in designing projects. What other adults can they recruit to cooperate with them—teachers, staff, parents, community businesspeople, others? Where can they find the materials or physical resources they need for the project? Or, how can they design a project to best use the resources they already have?

Flexibility

No project goes exactly as planned. Teachers must build in as much flexibility as possible to take advantage of unexpected resources or opportunities that become available or challenges that students will face.

Value the Work

It is important that the projects have intrinsic value other than the lessons they are designed to teach. They should provide goods or services that are of value. They may provide services that help to run the school or classroom or improve its information flow. Or they may provide a salable product or one that is of value beyond the school. This value helps students to take pride in what they are doing and provides motivation to do the project well.

Value the Youngster

Projects must start with the skills that students already have. Teachers and other adults involved in these projects must believe that students are able to perform at a high level. As the old saying goes, students will rise to your expectations. Teachers must be comfortable coaching students while allowing them to design and manage their own projects.

Connections with the Community

Build connections with the community by drawing in local businesspeople as consultants, employers, or resource providers. Some of the projects may involve students in work at a community organization outside the school. Others may draw on the community for clients. There are many benefits to such connections. They make the project possible, they get the community more involved with the school, and they expose students to aspects of their community they might not be familiar with.

Reflection

It is not enough for students to engage in these projects. Time must be set aside for them to think about what they did, why it did or did not work, what they learned from the activity, and where else they could apply what they learned. This puts the learning in context, increases its meaning to students, and increases the likelihood that the lessons learned will be transferred to other situations.

How To Develop an Individualized Career and Educational Plan

Teacher   High School   Career and Technical Education
                                                               Educational Technology
                                                               Family Engagement
                                                               Individualized Education

Introduction

This document is based on the simple premise that all students need to have an Individualized Career and Educational (ICE) Plan that is orderly, progressive over time, and cumulative (in terms of data). Information is the basis for good decision making; students need to take the most active part in the assimilation of aspects of career and educational self-assessment by which decisions can be made. Parents are expected to take an active and informed role in the development of their child's career and educational planning process. Counselors are the "navigators of the ship," that is, they assist the student and parents in the development of this planning document.

There are nine major aspects of this document that encompass these prescribed components. Additionally, we have included internet sites for continued research in career and educational planning. Finally, a student *activity time management plan* for Grades 9–12 is provided.

Please print the ICE Plan form from these pages. Create a portfolio and use each section of the ICE Plan as a divider. As you learn more about yourself, update your ICE Plan. As you gather other information—such as college catalogs, financial aid forms, etc.—place them in your portfolio. You need to have a place for all of your stuff. *You need to be the master of your own plan.*

Personal Data

Sometimes the best place to start is at the beginning, and if you look closely, the beginning says quite a bit about you. Take your name, for instance. What is the history of your name? Do you have a social security number? You will need it for financial aid purposes in the future and certainly when you begin work. Most people have a telephone number, but not everyone has an e-mail address. Do you know how to use e-mail? Exactly when do you expect to graduate? These are some reasons why you need to take a close look at the very basics.

Name _____ Date of birth _____ SSN _____

Address _____ City _____ State _____ Zip _____

Phone _____ E-mail address _____

Projected date of graduation _____

Name of closest relative _____

Address _____ Phone _____

Guidance counselor _____ Phone _____

Career and Educational Goals

If you can fill in this information right now, then go ahead and do it—we commend you for knowing so much about yourself. However, if you can't, skip it for now and go the resources at the end of this section. You may have to go to the Assessment Data section and begin to fill it out to get a handle on career and educational information to help you make career and educational goal statements.

Educational Goal 9th Grade Career Goal	Educational Goal 10th Grade Career Goal	Educational Goal 11th Grade Career Goal	Educational Goal 12th Grade Career Goal
Educational Goal	Educational Goal	Educational Goal	Educational Goal

Resources to help you with career goals:
- ◆ Career Search: College Board
- ◆ Not-So-Trivial Pursuit—Of Careers
- ◆ Discover Your Work
- ◆ *The Occupational Handbook*
- ◆ Military Career Guide Online

Resources to help you with educational goals:
- ◆ What Can I Do With A Degree In?
- ◆ Study Skills Check List
- ◆ College Search
- ◆ UC Pathways
- ◆ CSU Mentor

Assessment Data

You need to take an inventory of information about you—a personal profile so to speak, a snapshot of yourself. This personal profile is the foundation for all kinds of decisions; it is absolutely critical in helping you. Your counselor will help you to complete the data that the school has. You should know what you are good at right now and what matters most to you. How do you learn best? What is your career interest? Does your personality profile compare to your career interests? You should know or find out all there is to know about yourself; decisions are best made when you have information. What could be more important to you than to find out as much as possible about you?

Name of Inventory or Test	Date	Results
IDEAS		
SDS		
COPES		
Kiersey Bates		
ASVAB		
PSAT		
SAT I/SAT II		
Stanford Reading		
Stanford Math		
Stanford Writing		
IEP		

Resources to help you with your assessment data:
- How To Learn Anything Fast, www.howtolearn.com
- Know Your Personality Type, www.knowyourtype.com
- School Psychology Resources Online, www.schoolpsychology.net
- Holland Interest Inventory, jobs.esc.state.nc.us/planning/ela.htm
- Kiersey Temperament Sorter, www.kersey.com

Four-Year High School Plan

What are your post–high school plans? You need to determine that path early in your high school career. If you have the slightest inkling that you might go to college, then you need to cover your bases and make sure you take college preparatory courses.

Whatever path you decide on, you need to know two things: what courses are required and how many credits are needed for graduation. Pull out your student handbook and start planning.

High School Course Selection Plan

9th Grade	10th Grade	11th Grade	12th Grade
English	English	English	English
Math	Math	Math	Government, economics
Physical education	World history	American history	Computer elective
Drivers education, computer skills	Science	Science	Fine art

High School Graduation Requirements

English	Eight semesters
Mathematics	Six semesters—two may be taken outside the Math department
Social studies	Two semesters of world history, two semesters of U.S. history, one semester of government, and one semester of economics
Science	Two semesters of life science and two semesters of physical science
Physical education	Four semesters (marching band may substitute)
Fine art	Two semesters or world language
World language	Two semesters or fine art
Electives	220 units
Exams	Reading, writing, mathematics, spelling

Resources to help you with your four-year high school plan:
- High School Career Center
- UC Pathways
- Mentor
- College
- Community College

Interests

This section should never be left blank! You go to school, live in a community, and must like to do something! The whole point of this section is to become involved; leaving this section blank does not look very good.

Grade	School Activity	Community Activity	Interests and Hobbies
9			
10			
11			
12			

Employment History

There is dignity in all honest work. Many kids go to school full time and work 10, 20, and sometimes more hours per week. An acceptable and explainable (to college admission advisers) reason for not being able to fill the Interests section is that you work.

Employer/Address	Date(s) Employed	Responsibility

Career-Preparation Activities

You should not leave your career to chance. You need to engage yourself in activities that will provide you with valuable career-preparation information. Check one or more activities from the list below and research each activity. Your counselor or the Internet are good resources for getting the information you need. If you are going to any kind of postsecondary institution, you will probably need some kind of financial aid. Some people think that financial aid is only for four-year colleges. That is not true. You need to check out the postsecondary institution's financial aid office to make sure it qualifies for all federal and state aid programs.

- ♦ Enroll in a regional occupation program course that you are interested in.
- ♦ Learn how to market your experiences and abilities.
- ♦ Pursue on-the-job training through an apprenticeship or job fair.
- ♦ Enlist in the military.
- ♦ Attend a trade school or vocational school.
- ♦ Obtain financial aid.
- ♦ Attend a two-year college to prepare for work.
- ♦ Research schools that you are considering.

Post–High School Plans

Go ahead check off one or two if you like, but make a decision. Uncertainty will get you confused, and all you will do is to spin your wheels and wind up in a hole. You can change your mind at any time, but make a decision now! As a matter of fact, some very smart people who study career development say that people will change their careers as many as four or five times during their lifetime.

Employment:
- ☐ Full-time job
- ☐ Part-time job
- ☐ Military

Education:
- ☐ Vocational or technical
- ☐ Apprenticeship
- ☐ On-the-job-training
- ☐ Community college
- ☐ Four-year college or university

Résumé and Recommendations

Continue to work on your relationships with your teachers, employers, supervisors, and those who can write a letter of recommendation for you. Remember, the more they know you, the better they can write a letter.

In addition, continue to work on your résumé. Seek help from your English teacher and online services. (For college application essays and résumé cover letters, see www.editmenow.com.)

School–Community Collaboration

When all groups in a community provide collective support to the school, a strong infrastructure sustains a caring, supportive environment in which youth can thrive and achieve. The following tools are included in this chapter:

How Do You Get the Community Involved in Helping to Address At-Risk Youth, Truancy, and Dropout Prevention?

Community Development Framework for Truancy and Dropout Prevention.

Indicators of School and Community Readiness for the Prevention of Truancy and School Dropouts.

Community Development Framework for Truancy and Dropout Prevention.

School and Community Indicators for the Ongoing Assessment of Truancy and Dropout Prevention.

I am indebted to Fran Weinbaum, former coordinator of the Vermont Consortium for Successful High School Completion, for designing this tool and for making me aware of these assessment tools.

How Do You Get the Community Involved in Helping to Address At-Risk Youth, Truancy, and Dropout Prevention?

Administrator   All Grade Levels   Family Engagement
Teacher   Professional Development
                                                                     Safe Learning Environments
                                                                  School–Community Collaboration

According to Fran Weinbaum, "Schools cannot address the issue of at-risk youth, truancy and dropout prevention by themselves. The Vermont Department of Education is aware of the need to get the community involved in aiding the state's schools in creating a bond between school and the community."

Fran Weinbaum, former coordinator of the Vermont Consortium for Successful High School Completion, wrote, "once a school with its community identifies the underlying conditions that are contribution to truancy and dropouts, then they begin looking at strategies to meet those specific needs." I am indebted to her for designing the following tool and for making me aware of these assessment tools.

Figure 13.1 Community Development Framework for Truancy and Dropout Prevention (Theory of Change Planning Guide used with the Community Development Indicators)

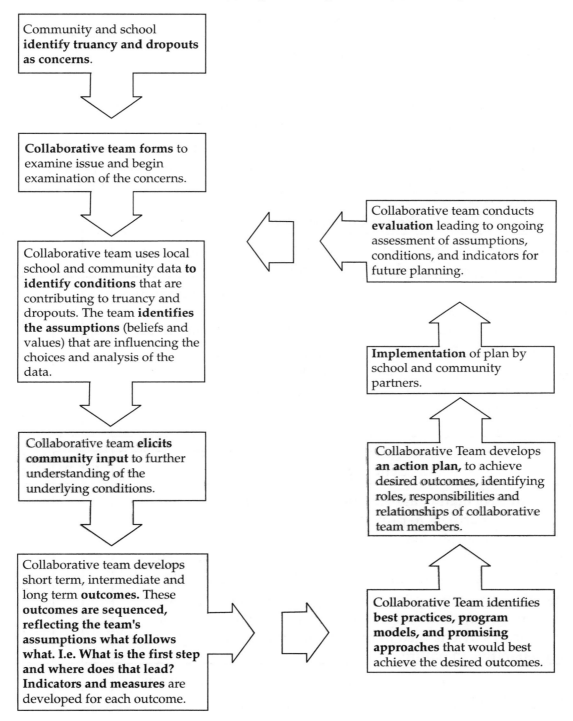

Community and school **identify truancy and dropouts as concerns**.

Collaborative team forms to examine issue and begin examination of the concerns.

Collaborative team uses local school and community data **to identify conditions** that are contributing to truancy and dropouts. The team **identifies the assumptions** (beliefs and values) that are influencing the choices and analysis of the data.

Collaborative team **elicits community input** to further understanding of the underlying conditions.

Collaborative team develops short term, intermediate and long term **outcomes**. These **outcomes are sequenced, reflecting the team's assumptions what follows what. I.e. What is the first step and where does that lead? Indicators and measures** are developed for each outcome.

Collaborative team conducts **evaluation** leading to ongoing assessment of assumptions, conditions, and indicators for future planning.

Implementation of plan by school and community partners.

Collaborative Team develops **an action plan,** to achieve desired outcomes, identifying roles, responsibilities and relationships of collaborative team members.

Collaborative Team identifies **best practices, program models, and promising approaches** that would best achieve the desired outcomes.

Indicators of School and Community Readiness for the Prevention of Truancy and School Dropouts

Response Key

1	No action has been taken on this indicator.
2	We are beginning to address this indicator.
3	Our school and community has developed a strategy to address this indicator, and we have made substantial progress toward implementation.
4	Our school and community has fully adopted a strategy to address this indicator, and we are continually adjusting the implementation plan to improve its impact on youth success in school and in the community.

Youth Engagement	1	2	3	4
Young people are involved in all aspects of collaborative work, including leadership and decision making.				
Youth representation includes students at risk of truancy and dropout, out-of-school youth, student leaders, students in alternative educational programs, and students who are in the regular school program.				
Youth are invited to partner with adults to plan and carry out meetings; are invited to training events for skill development; and are visible participants and leaders in all aspects of the task force's work.				

School Structure	1	2	3	4
There are articulation agreements between schools and community partners to provide multiple pathways and flexible schedules for all students; for career awareness and development; for students' personal health and social needs; and for informing and supporting the educational process.				
Attendance and discipline policies, protocols, and procedures identify students who are at risk, provide opportunities for students to stay engaged in their education, and are supportive and reparative in nature.				
Student, parents, and faculty and staff have input into review and development.				

There is mutual respect between all school community members, the school is safe for everyone, and all feel welcome at any time.				
Best practices* in student learning and performance, learning environments, policy, funding and governance, youth engagement, and parent and community involvement are promoted, implemented, and evaluated schoolwide.				
There is connection and continuity between grade levels in planning for student success.				
Academic and career education are integrated for all students.				

Leadership	1	2	3	4
Superintendents, school principals, and civic leaders bring current information to the school board, school faculty and staff, students, parents, community partners, and community at large about the nature and scope of the problem and the need for action.				
School and community leaders support and participate in local collaborative efforts toward school success.				
Available school Pre-K–16 and community data and reports are shared with all school personnel, school boards, students, parents, community leaders, and members at large.				
Anecdotal information, such as data from exit interviews, is available in an appropriate manner.				
Discussions are held as to the significance of the data. Underlying conditions that are contributing to the problems are identified.				
An array of services and opportunities, including prevention, early identification and support, and extensive support, are available to students and their families.				
Plans exist to meet gaps in services and opportunities.				
Partnerships between educational providers are developed to support options for students.				

Planning	1	2	3	4
The collaborative effort is coordinated with other educational and youth initiatives; these initiatives are represented on the collaborative, or there are regular updates about each other's work; joint efforts are undertaken whenever possible.				
The collaborative work is directly connected to other school improvement plans and activities. Programs and activities are aligned with the school's action plan and with existing community youth service plans.				
The selection of programs and activities is related to identified conditions with clear outcomes and measures.**				
System and program design and decision making are informed by available data and ongoing evaluation.				
The collaborative is involved in establishing outcomes and success indicators.				
There is a plan for program review and evaluation that is based on process outcomes and student data.				
There is a joint school and community strategic plan for school success for all students that outlines the means for systemic, programmatic, and financial sustainability.				

Community Engagement	1	2	3	4
The community actively supports education for all children and youth by participating in committees and forums; participating in apprenticeship, service learning, and mentoring programs; actively participating in the schools (parent and/or volunteer); and supporting the financial needs of the schools through budget processes and fund-raising efforts to provide the scope of programs needed for student success.				
Community members value the contributions of youth, believe in their worth, provide opportunities and resources for them, and provide opportunities for youth engagement and decision making and leadership, specifically in issues related to young people but also in other civic concerns.				

Notes:

* See *High Schools on the Move: Renewing Vermont's Commitment to Secondary Education,* Vermont Department of Education, 2002; www.state.st.us/educ/cwd/hsi. See also *Making the Difference: Research and Practice in Community Schools,* Coalition for Community Schools, 2003; www.communityschool.org. For guidelines on engaging youth as partners, see William Lofquist, *The Technology of Development Workbook,* Development Publications, 1998; the National Youth Development Information Center, www.nydic.org; and the National Service Learning Clearinghouse, www.servicelearning.org.

** See Vermont Agency of Human Services, *Outcome-Based Planning 2002: What Works* series, www.ahs.state.vt.us/AHSOutcIndic.htm. For information on theory of change, contact David Murphey, Senior Policy Analyst, Vermont Agency of Human Services, at davidm@wpgate1.ahs.state.vt.us. See the Vermont Department of Employment and Training, Crosswalk of Youth Programs and Services, 2002; Contact: Greg Voorheis, gvoorheis@det.state.vt.us.

Community Development Framework
for Truancy and Dropout Prevention

School/community _____

Completed by_____Date _____ Phone/e-mail _____

Indicators of School–Community Readiness
for the Prevention of Truancy and School Dropouts

Recognition (R) of the problems of truancy and school dropouts and *leadership* (L) of the issues by

_____Superintendent	_____Community partners
_____School administration	_____Civic leaders/business
_____School boards/SU	_____Parents
_____School boards/high school	_____Students
_____School boards/elementary	_____School faculty and staff

Comments:

Broad-based collaborative group formed to look at the issues with representation from (check groups represented)

☐ Students	☐ Social services
☐ School board	☐ Vocational rehabilitation
☐ Parents	☐ Substance abuse treatment/prevention
☐ Parent child center	☐ Youth employment programs
☐ Early education	☐ Funding organizations
☐ Elementary education	☐ Corrections/probation and parole
☐ Middle school	☐ Local community, including businesses
☐ High School	☐ Diversion/reparative justice programs
☐ Higher education	☐ Regional partnership
☐ Adult literacy and education	☐ Local law enforcement
☐ Youth and family service organizations	☐ Community Justice Center
☐ Teen health providers	☐ Courts and judges

☐ Alternative education   ☐ Mental health

☐ Vocational and technical   ☐ Others _____
education

Comments:

Task Force Development

Please respond to the following statements with "Yes" (this is true) "UD" (this is actively being worked on), or "No" (this is not true).

_____   The collaborative group has a stated vision and mission for its work.
Comments:

_____   The collaborative group has a clear and articulated governance structure and decision-making process.
Comments:

_____   The collaborative group has identified and is well versed in a planning model that focuses on the conditions and root causes rather than the symptoms of the identified issues.
Comments:

_____   Research-based strategies and promising approaches that relate to the identified conditions and desired outcomes have been identified.
Comments:

_____   The collaborative group broadens its membership as different issues are addressed.
Comments:

_____   The collaborative group links effectively with other initiatives, groups. and organizations that are working with and on the behalf of youth and education.
Comments:

_____   The collaborative group has resources to support its work.
Comments:

_____   Members of the collaborative group contribute to support the group's work, financially or in kind.

Comments:

_____   Community involvement is encouraged through forums, study circles, focus groups, invitations to meetings, subcommittees, and communication of the group's work through local and school newspapers, newsletters, and media.

Comments:

Youth Engagement

Youth Engagement	Exploration	Transition	Full Implementation	Comments
Youth engagement as partners	Young people are not included in discussions and decisions school and community issues.	Young people are asked for their input and ideas but are not given decision-making power or leadership roles.	Young people are involved in all aspects of collaborative work, including leadership and decision making.	
Youth representation is diverse	Youth representation is limited to one group of young people (for example, student leaders).	Youth representation from diverse groups is sought.	Youth representation includes students at risk of truancy and dropout, out-of- school youth, students in alternative educational programs, and students who are in the regular school program.	
Youth leadership development	Youth members are not given the opportunity to learn and practice leadership skills.	Youth are participants in meetings and are given limited opportunity to lead meet-ings with adults assuming most of the responsibility.	Youth are invited to partner with adults to plan and carry out meetings; are invited to training events for skill development; and are visible participants and leaders in all aspects of the task force's work.	

School Structure

School Structure	Exploration	Transition	Full Implementation	Comments
School–community partnerships for academic and social and personal health	Schools and community partnerships do not exist.	School–community partnerships exist to meet the needs of individual students; for specific demographic student groups; or for specific events.	There are articulation agreements between schools and community partners to provide multiple pathways and flexible schedules for all students; for career awareness and development; for students' personal health and social needs; and for informing and supporting the educational process.	
Attendance and discipline	Attendance and discipline policies, protocols, and procedures are punitive and exclude students from educational programs.	Attendance and discipline policies, protocols, and procedures are examined for ways to keep students engaged in their education and to be reparative rather than punitive in nature.	Attendance and discipline policies, protocols, and procedures identify students who are at risk, provide opportunities for students to stay engaged in their education, and are supportive and reparative in nature.	
School	The school climate is not respectful, welcoming or safe for all students, staff, parents, or community members.	Students, staff, parents, and community feel respected, welcome, and safe in some situations and activities in school.	There is mutual respect between all school community members, the school is safe for everyone, and all feel welcome at any time.	
Best practices	Best practices* in student learning and performance, learning environments, policy, funding and governance, and parent and community involvement are not recognized by the school or part of their strategic planning. Individual teachers may employ some best practices.	Best practices* in student learning and performance, learning environments, policy, funding and governance, and parent and community involvement are recognized but not fully implemented or not implemented as part of a strategic plan for the entire school.	Best practices* in student learning and performance, learning environments, policy, funding and governance, and parent and community involvement are promoted, implemented, and evaluated schoolwide. There is connection and continuity between grade levels in planning for student success.	

* See *High Schools on the Move: Renewing Vermont's Commitment to Secondary Education 2002 Vermont Department of Education.*

Community Engagement

Community Engagement	Exploration	Transition	Full Implementation	Comments
Community value of education	The community does not value education for all children and youth. ("Community" refers to individuals of all ages and groups, such as civic groups, community organizations, funding organizations, and business associations.)	The community recognizes the importance of education but does not actively support the scope of programs necessary to meet the local students' needs.	The community actively supports education for all children and youth by participating in committees and forums; participating in apprenticeship, service-learning, and mentoring programs; actively participating in the schools (parent and/or volunteer); and supporting the financial needs of the schools through budget processes and fund-raising efforts to provide the scope of programs needed for student success.	
Community perception of youth	Community members do not engage youth directly except in the delivery of services. Youth are not invited to meetings to discuss issues pertaining to them.	Community members ask about the perceptions of youth but do not actively engage them as partners. Community members' connections with youth are limited.	Community members value the contributions of youth, believe in their worth, provide opportunities and resources for them, and provide opportunities for youth involvement and leadership, specifically in issues related to young people but also in other civic concerns.	

Leadership

Leadership	Exploration	Transition	Full Implementation	Comments
Leadership for truancy and dropout prevention	School or community leaders do not state concern about truancy and dropout prevention or make it a priority.	School or community leaders articulate their concern in meetings with school personnel, school boards, and community partners.	Superintendents, school principals, and civic leaders bring current information to the school board, school faculty and staff, students, parents, community partners, and community at large about the nature and scope of the problem and the need for action.	
Data and reports are used to substantiate the nature and scope of the problem	Available data and reports are not shared or examined in a way that promotes understanding of the problem.	Available data and reports are shared and examined with school faculty, staff, and school boards.	Available data are shared with all school personnel, school boards, students, parents, community leaders, and members at large. Anecdotal information, such as data from exit interviews, is available in an appropriate manner. Discussions are held as to the meaning and significance of the data. Underlying conditions that are contributing to the problems are identified.	
There is an array of services and opportunities in the school and the community that support school success for all students.	Available services and opportunities are not generally known or accessible.	Available services are known and gaps in services are identified. Coordination between services occurs for individual students.	An array of services and opportunities, including prevention, early identification and support, and extensive support, are available to students and their families. Plans exist to meet gaps in services/opportunities.	

Planning

Planning	Exploration	Transition	Full Implementation	Comments
Task force work is connected to other educational and youth service initiatives	The task force is aware of other initiatives.	The task force is gathering information about the nature and scope of other educational and youth service initiatives and the possible connections.	The task force work coordinates with other educational and youth initiatives; these initiatives are represented on the task force or there is regular updating about each other's work; joint efforts are undertaken whenever possible. The task force's work is directly	
Program planning and development is based in identified conditions that contribute to truancy and dropouts	The selection of programs and activities is not related to identified conditions.	There is some examination of underlying conditions, but the selection of programs and activities is largely symptom based or funding driven.	The selection of programs and activities is related to identified conditions with clear outcomes and measures.** Programs and activities are aligned with the school's action plan and with existing community youth service plans.	
Evaluation informs program design and decision making	Program design and decision making do not reflect available evaluation results and data. Programs are not fully evaluated.	Data and evaluation results are available but are not used effectively in program design or decision making.	System and program design and decision making are informed by available data and ongoing evaluation. There is a plan for program review and evaluation that is based on process outcomes and student data.	
Sustainability of programs	School and community do not know what programs are effective and do not have a plan for ongoing support and funding.	School and community can demonstrate what activities and programs are effective but do not have a sustainability plan.	There is a school and community strategic plan for programmatic and financial sustainability of effective programs and activities.	

** See Vermont Agency of Human Services, *Outcome Based Planning 2002: What Works* series. See also the Vermont Department of Employment and Training, Crosswalk of Youth Programs and Services, 2002.

School and Community Indicators
for the Ongoing Assessment of Truancy and Dropout Prevention

Please place a check in the box following each statement that most closely represents your perception of each item in your school and community. Use the key below to guide your choices.

Date of completion _____ School/community _____

Role/position _____ Name (optional) _____

Response Key

1	This indicator is not represented in current practices.
2	The community and school are learning more about this indicator through data and examining current practices and research based models.
3	The community and school have developed a strategy to address this indicator.
4	The community and school are implementing strategies to address this indicator.
5	The community and school are continually examining outcomes related to this indicator and refining plans to increase outcomes.

Leadership	1	2	3	4	5
Superintendents, school principals, and civic leaders bring current information to the school board, school faculty and staff, students, parents, community partners, and community at large about the nature and scope of the truancy and dropout problem and the need for action.					
School and community leaders support and participate in local collaborative efforts for school success.					
Available Pre-K–12 plus postsecondary school and community data and reports are shared with all school personnel, school boards, students, parents, community leaders, and members at large.					
Qualitative and quantitative data about the truancy and dropout problem, such as summary statements from exit interviews with students who have left school, and focus groups are available in an appropriate manner.					
Discussions with all partners are held to determine the significance of the data.					

School leaders advocate an array of school and community services and opportunities, including prevention, early identification and support, and extensive support, that are available to students and their families.					
Partnerships between educational providers are developed to support options for students.					
School and district leadership takes initiative in developing and changing procedures and policies as needed to support truancy and drop out prevention efforts.					
What you would add?					

Planning	1	2	3	4	5
There is a vision of student success—skills, knowledge, and attitudes that students need to have when they graduate from high school to be successful in college, employment, or training—that has been created collaboratively by the school and community.					
Truancy and dropout-prevention efforts are coordinated with other educational and youth initiatives; these initiatives are represented in planning or there is regular updating about each other's work; joint efforts are undertaken whenever possible.					
Truancy and dropout prevention is connected directly to other K–12 school improvement plans and activities. Programs and activities are aligned with the school's action plan and with existing community youth service plans.					
The selection of programs and activities is related to identified conditions, existing resources, and gaps in services, with clear outcomes and measures.					
The system program design and decision making are informed by available data and ongoing evaluation.					
Indicators of outcome and success are established collaboratively with a broad range of partners and constituencies in the school and in the community.					
What would you add?					

Youth Engagement	1	2	3	4	5
Young people are involved in all aspects of truancy and dropout- prevention planning, including leadership and decision making.					
Youth representation includes students at risk of truancy and dropout, out-of-school youth, student leaders, students in alternative educational programs, and students who are in the regular school program.					
Youth are invited to partner with adults to plan and carry out meetings; are invited to training events for skill development; and are visible participants and leaders in all aspects of the task force's work.					
Adult–youth relationships are encouraged through opportunities such as teacher advisories and mentoring. Adults are provided training, supervision, and support for these roles.					
Youth are given opportunities to mentor or tutor younger students through structured supervised programs. Youth receive training for these roles.					
Youth civic engagement is recognized as a critical component of education. School time, structure, and academic credit support youth engagement in changing things that matter to them in their schools and communities.					
What you would add?					

Community Engagement	1	2	3	4	5
The community actively supports education for all children and youth. This is evident through participation in committees and forums; participation in apprenticeship, service learning, and mentoring programs; active participation in the schools (parent and/or volunteer); support of the financial needs of the schools through budget processes and fund-raising efforts to provide the scope of programs needed for student success.					
Community members value the contributions of youth, believe in their worth, provide opportunities and resources for them, and provide opportunities for youth engagement and decision making and leadership, specifically in issues related to young people but also in other civic concerns.					
Community members and organizations have information about and an opportunity to discuss the effect of local and global economic and social impacts on local education.					
What you would add?					

School Structure	1	2	3	4	5
There are articulation agreements between schools and community partners to provide multiple pathways and flexible schedules for all students; for career awareness and development; for students' personal health and social needs; and for informing and supporting the educational process.					
Attendance and discipline policies, protocols, and procedures identify students who are at risk, provide opportunities for students to stay engaged in their education, and are supportive and reparative in nature.					
A reparative approach to discipline holds students accountable for their actions while engaging them in addressing the conditions that contributed to the discipline problem.					
Students, parents, and faculty and staff have input into the review and development of school programs and initiatives.					
There is mutual respect among all members of the school community, the school is safe for everyone, and all feel welcome at any time.					
Faculty and staff have time and support, including professional development where indicated, to collaboratively examine and discuss student work, student data, teaching, and schoolwide practices and procedures for the purpose of improving student learning.					
Best practices in student learning and performance, learning environments, policy, funding and governance, youth engagement, and parent and community involvement are promoted, implemented, and evaluated schoolwide.					
School policies and procedures support credit-earning community-based learning, including internships, apprenticeships, co-op programs, service learning, independent study, and community service.					
There is connection and continuity between grade levels in planning for student success. Transitions between grades, particularly between school levels, are supported academically and socially.					
Academic and career planning and preparation are provided for all students.					
What you would add?					

Safe Learning Environments

A comprehensive violence-prevention plan, including conflict resolution, must deal with potential violence as well as crisis management. A safe learning environment provides daily experiences, at all grade levels, that enhance positive social attitudes and effective interpersonal skills. The following tools are included in this chapter:

What Are the Warning Signs of Youth Suicide? developed by Franklin P. Schargel.

How to Develop an Effective Strategy to Counter Bullying in Schools, from "Bullying in Schools," U.S. Department of Justice, Community Oriented Police Services (COPS), www.cops.usdoj.gov.

How to Encourage Students to Think about Staying in School, developed by the Chicago Public Schools.

Keeping Kids Safe: Helping Kids Face Tough Issues, developed by the National Crime Prevention Council, Joselle Alexander, Assistant Director, Children and Youth Initiatives; 1000 Connecticut Avenue NW, 13th Floor, Washington, DC 20036, www.ncpc.org. Used with permission.

What Are the Warning Signs of Youth Suicide?

Administrator
Counselor
Special Educator
Teacher

Middle School
High School

Family Engagement
Individual Instruction
Professional Development
Safe Learning Environments

Suicide is among the three top causes of youth death. Almost as many teens die from suicide as the 4th–10th leading causes of death combined. Those who are at risk are more likely to relieve their frustration of school failure by choosing suicide.

Although no one single symptom—or even a combination of factors—is a predictor of suicide, the following list reports the most prevalent causes of youth suicide. The greater the number of warning signs, the greater the likelihood of suicide. If you suspect that a student is suicidal, teachers and students should tell a counselor or an administrator.

Warning Signs

The youth who is most at risk of attempting suicide is one who shows the following signs:

- Has made previous suicide attempts

- Talks about committing suicide
- Feels that "it is all my fault"

- Exhibits anger

- Exhibits serious depression, moodiness, hopelessness, or withdrawal
- Is a loner

- Increases use of drugs or alcohol

- Changes sleeping or eating habits

- Experiences turmoil within the family (divorce, remarriage, separation, merging of two families)
- Has a family history of suicide
- Has had a recent stressful event or loss
- Has easy access to lethal methods, especially guns
- Exhibits rebellious behavior or runs away

- Has difficulty concentrating or shows a decline in the quality of schoolwork
- Loses interest in previously pleasurable activities
- Gives verbal hints, such as "I won't be a problem for you much longer" or "Nothing matters"

- Cries often

- Exhibits chronic or sudden truancy
- Gives away possessions
- Has experienced the recent suicide of a loved one or family member
- Is preoccupied with death and dying
- Loses interest in personal appearance

- Has conflicts around sexual orientation
- Experienced a romantic breakup
- Has access to firearms
- Experiences increased pressure to perform, achieve, or be responsible
- Takes unnecessary risks

The greater the number of warning signs, the greater the risk.

How To Develop an Effective Strategy to Counter Bullying in Schools

Administrator   All Grade Levels   Professional Development
Teacher   Safe Learning Environments
Family Engagement   School–Community Collaboration

The following approaches can be used to address bullying:

♦ **Enlist the school principal's commitment and involvement.** The school principal's commitment to and involvement in addressing school bullying are key. A principal who invests the time and energy to tackle the problem collaboratively and comprehensively generally will get the most effective results.

♦ **Use a multifaceted, comprehensive approach.** A multifaceted, comprehensive approach includes the following:

  • Establishing a schoolwide policy that addresses indirect bullying (e.g., rumor spreading, isolation, social exclusion), which is more hidden, as well as direct bullying (e.g., physical aggression)

  • Providing guidelines for teachers, staff, and students (including witnesses) on specific actions to take if bullying occurs

  • Educating and involving parents so that they understand the problem, recognize its signs, and intervene appropriately

  • Adopting specific strategies to deal with individual bullies and victims, including meeting with their parents

  • Encouraging students to report known bullying

  • Developing a comprehensive reporting system to track bulling and the interventions use with specific bullies and victims

  • Encouraging students to be helpful to classmates who may be bullied

  • Developing tailored strategies to counter bullying in specific school hot spots, such as using environmental redesign, increasing supervision (by teachers, other staff members, parents, or volunteers), or using technological monitoring equipment

  • Conducting postintervention surveys to assess the impact of the strategies on school bullying

Specific Responses to Reduce Bullying in Schools

♦ **Use the "whole-school" approach.** The whole-school approach is somewhat easier to implement in elementary schools because of their size and structure. Because students generally interact with only one or two teachers a year, there are more consistent messages from teachers to students. Research tells us that the whole-school approach requires renewed effort each year (reinforcing antibullying strategies with returning students, their parents, and school staff). One-time efforts are less effective. Schools must prepare themselves to maintain momentum for antibullying initiatives year after year.

♦ **Increase student reporting of bullying.** To address the problem of students' resistance to reporting bullying, some schools have set up a bully hotline. Some schools use a "bully box": Students drop a note in the box to alert teachers and administrators to problem bullies.

♦ **Develop activities in less-supervised areas.** In these areas (e.g., schoolyards, lunchrooms), trained supervisors spot bullying and initiate activities that limit opportunities for it.

♦ **Reduce the amount of time students can spend unsupervised.** Because much bullying occurs during the least supervised time (e.g., recess, lunch breaks, class changes), reducing the amount of time available to students can reduce the amount of bullying.

♦ **Stagger recess, lunch, and class-release times.** This approach minimizes the number of bullies and victims present at one time, so supervisors have less trouble spotting bullying. However, supervisors must be mindful that most bullies are in the same grade as their victims.

♦ **Monitor areas where bullying can be expected,** such as bathrooms. Adult monitoring can increase the risk that bullies will get caught but may require increased staffing or trained volunteers.

♦ **Assign bullies to a particular location or to particular chores during release times.** This approach separates bullies from their intended victims. Some teachers give bullies constructive tasks to occupy them during release times. Careful victim monitoring is required to ensure that bullies do not pick on victims at other times.

♦ **Post classroom signs prohibiting bullying and listing the consequences.** This puts would-be bullies on notice and outlines the risks they are taking. Teacher must consistently enforce the rules for them to have meaning. Schools should post signs in each classroom and apply age-appropriate penalties.

♦ **Provide teachers with effective classroom-management training.** To address bullying, schools should ensure that all teachers have effective classroom-management training. Because research suggests that classes containing students with behavioral, emotional, or learning problems have more bullies and victims, teachers in those classes may require additional, tailored training in spotting and handling bullying.

◆ **Have high-level school administrators inform late-enrolling students and their parents about the school's bullying policy.** This removes any excuse new students have for bullying, puts parents on notice that the school takes bullying seriously, and stresses the importance the school places on countering it.

Responses with Limited Effectiveness

◆ **Training students in conflict resolution and peer mediation.** Research has shown that a number of schools that adopt conflict-resolution and peer-mediation training to address bullying (and other problems) are not successful because bullying involves the harassment of children with less power (rather than a conflict between peers of relatively equal status) by more powerful children.

◆ **Adopting a zero-tolerance policy.** Some schools, in their rush to "do something" about bullying, adopt a zero-tolerance policy against it without an in-depth analysis of the specific problem or the comprehensive involvement of administrators, teachers, other staff, student witnesses, parents, bullies, and victims at the school, class, and individual level. This approach may result in a high level of suspensions without full comprehension of how behavior needs to and can be changed. It does not solve the problem of the bully, who typically spends more unsupervised time in the home or the community if he or she is suspended or expelled. Zero tolerance also may have a chilling effect on the reporting of bullying.

◆ **Providing group therapy for bullies.** Some schools provide self-esteem training for bullies. This may be misdirected; research suggests that most bullies do not lack self-esteem.

◆ **Encouraging victims to simply stand up to bullies.** Without adequate support or adult involvement, this strategy may be harmful and physically dangerous for a victim of bullying.

How To Encourage Students To Think about Staying in School

Administrator   Middle School   Alternative Schooling
Counselor   High School   Family Engagement
Special Educator   Safe Learning Environments
Teacher

At-risk children frequently take the easy way out and drop out of school. The Chicago Public Schools developed a contract that all students and their parents must sign in order to drop out of school.

Consent to Withdraw from School

I, _____, acknowledge that by dropping out of school, I am voluntarily giving away my educational rights, privileges, and opportunities.

- I will be less likely to find good jobs that pay well, bad jobs that don't pay well, or maybe any job.
- I will not be able to afford many things that I will see others acquiring.
- I will be more likely to get caught up in criminal activity and illegal behavior.
- I will be more likely to spend time in jail or prison.
- I will be more likely to rely on the state welfare system for my livelihood.
- I will not have many choices about where to live.
- I will be considerably less able to properly care for and educate my children.

I, _____, confirm that I am over the age of 16. I have read and fully understand the consequences of dropping out of school, yet I choose to withdraw from school.

Student's signature _____

I, _____, confirm that my child is over the age of 16. I fully understand the consequences of my child dropping out of school, yet I will allow my child to withdraw from school.

Parent or guardian's signature _____

The above-named individuals have been fully informed of the consequences of dropping out of school. I have informed them of alternative and adult educational services that are available in the community.

Principal's signature _____

It's not too late to stay in school

Keeping Kids Safe:
Helping Kids Face Tough Issues

Administrator   All Grade Levels   Family Involvement
Counselor   Professional Development
Special Educator   Safe Learning Environments
Teacher

The National Crime Prevention Council has developed a matrix to help children, their parents, and educators address the tough issues that children face today.

Keeping Kids Safe: Helping Children Face Tough Issues

	Alcohol, Tobacco, and Drugs	Bullying	Conflict Management Diversity	Diversity
Defining the issue	The percentage of young people who say they have used alcohol, tobacco, and drugs is down. Prevention education is working, but we can't stop teaching about this issue.	Bullying can be physical or social-emotional. It is characterized by an imbalance of power. It consists of repeated, systematic harassment by an individual or group.	Conflicts can be rooted in resources, needs, values, or perceptions. Conflict can be managed by addressing anger, communicating effectively, and problem solving.	Culture is a set of values and rules of behavior. Hate crimes (crimes committed against someone who is different) range from property damage to threats and assault. Gender-based harassment is any unwanted and unwelcome sexual behavior.
Significance of the problem	According to the Substance Abuse and Mental Health Services Administration, in 2001, 56 percent of 12-17-year-olds said it's very or fairly easy to obtain marijuana. Young people use drugs to have fun and feel good, fit in and belong, imitate older people, take risks, and satisfy curiosity.	Every day, 160,000 children miss school for fear of bullying. Sixty-one percent of students report witnessing bullying or taunting at least once a day (National Crime Prevention Council, 2003).	Fifty-six percent of fourth and fifth graders report being hit by a peer; one-third say they would hit back (Journal of School Health, 2002). Ten percent of secondary school teachers and 8 percent of elementary school teachers report being threatened by a student (U.S. Department of Education, 2002).	More than thirteen percent of students ages 12-18 report being called a hate-related word at school. (National Center for Educational Statistics, 2002) Eighty-three percent of girls and seventy-nine percent of boys report experiencing gender-based harassment in schools. (American Association of University Women, 2001)
What you can do—Teach children and youth to…	Have fun and relieve stress without alcohol or drugs. Make friends and resist negative peer pressure. Identify the consequences of using alcohol or drugs (harm body, disappoint parents, do poorly in school, etc.). Make responsible decisions.	If they are bullied, tell the person to stop, walk away, avoid or ignore the teasing, make a joke, hang with friends, tell an adult. If they witness someone being bullied, help the person get away, recognize bullying behaviors, get an adult, recruit others to help the person, befriend the person, and speak up.	Recognize what makes them angry and manage anger by calming their body, redirecting energy, or getting away. State clearly how they feel and what they want. Listen attentively to others. Solve problems by identifying the issue, brainstorming solutions, agreeing upon a solution, and following through with the decision.	Avoid teasing or excluding anyone on the basis of religion, race, etc. because it is wrong. Identify gender-based harassment and tell an adult if they experience it. Recognize the similarities and differences among people. Appreciate how differences enhance a group.
What you can do—Additional steps	Let them know you disapprove of using alcohol and drugs. Talk with them to build a trusting relationship. Be involved in their lives; know their friends and hobbies. Ask questions when they go out. Make rules and enforce them consistently. Model responsible behavior.	Be watchful—supervise young people on the playground, at bus stops, etc. Tell them that bullying is unacceptable. Reassure them and tell them they were right to talk to you about bullying problems. Work with other adults to help those who are bullied and those who bully others.	Model these behaviors for managing anger, communicating, and problem solving. Share how you have managed conflicts you have faced. Intervene if children need to cool off or if they need help working through the problem-solving process.	Expose young people to different cultures. Remind them that there are many ways of seeing things. Acknowledge young people's questions and answer them directly. Allow them to develop their talents. Refrain from making prejudiced comments or assumptions based on stereotypes.

	Home Alone	Internet	Media Influences	Neighborhood Safety—Stranger Awareness
Defining the issue	After school, children may be supervised by a parent, placed in an after-school program, or left home alone. Children need to know emergency information, safety rules, and what to do if they ever find a gun.	Fifty-nine percent of young people ages 5–17 use the Internet (Benton Foundation, 2000). Young people use the Internet to send e-mail, research projects, visit chat rooms, instant message, and play games.	Violence in the media can occur with weapons, without weapons, or with explosions and crashes. Advertising shows products to be fun, used by everyone, able to satisfy personal desires, used by famous people or models, and better than other products.	Not all strangers are dangerous. Not all known adults are safe. There are three types of abductions—family, acquaintance, and stranger.
Significance of the problem	Eight million children ages 5–14 regularly spend time without adult supervision (National Institute on Out-of-School Time, 2003). Thirty-five percent of households own at least one gun (Johns Hopkins Center for Gun Policy and Research, 1999).	Risks online include exposure to inappropriate material, bullying and harassment, intent of physical molestation, and legal and financial issues (scams). Almost 20 percent of youth have received sexual solicitations online (National Center for Missing and Exploited Children, 2000).	Viewing violent media can cause increased aggressive behavior, increased fear of victimization, desensitization, and increased desire for more violence. Advertising techniques parallel the reasons why young people use alcohol and drugs.	In 1999, 262,100 children were abducted—78 percent by family members and 22 percent by nonfamily members (Office of Juvenile Justice and Delinquency Prevention, 2002). Of nonfamily abductions, 53 percent were by known adults and 45 percent were by strangers (Office of Juvenile Justice and Delinquency Prevention, 2002). Sexual assault, physical assault, and robbery are associated with kidnappings.
What you can do— Teach children and youth	Contact you, a relative, or neighbor if they need help. Dial 911 or 0 if there is an emergency. Tell their complete name, address, and phone number to an operator. Follow a safety routine—take a safe route home, go to a safe spot if things don't look right at home, call someone to check in, and follow a schedule of activities. Let the answering machine pick up if anyone calls; never answer the door to strangers. React if they see a gun—stop, don't touch, get away, tell a trusted grown-up.	Never give out personal information to anyone they meet online. Never agree to a face-to-face meeting with someone met online without discussing it with their parents. Get a parent's permission before entering a chat room. Tell a trusted adult if they encounter anything that makes them scared or uncomfortable.	Distinguish between fantasy and reality; understand the real consequences of violence that may not be shown in the media. Identify types of media violence and how they feel when they see it. Distinguish between needs and wants. Identify advertising techniques. Determine whether a product can do everything the advertisement claims.	Identify potentially dangerous situations. Say "no" if they are in a dangerous situation, "go" to a safe place, "yell" for help, and "tell" a trusted adult about what happened. Always check with a caregiver before going anywhere with anyone. Stick with friends when playing outside. Trust their instincts and talk to an adult or go to a safe spot if they ever feel scared.
What you can do— Additional steps	Leave emergency contact information by the phone. Distinguish between emergencies and nonemergencies and who young people can call. Role play situations—calling 911, what to do if the phone rings or if someone knocks at the door. If you own a gun, keep it unloaded, locked up, and out of children's reach.	Ask young people what they do online. Go online with them. Keep the computer in a family room. Consider blocking software. Don't post pictures of children online. Report any concerns to your internet service provider or the Cyber Tipline (800-843-5678).	Monitor or limit the media that young people can use. Watch television or movies with them and discuss any violence shown. Contact networks to advocate for nonviolent shows. Talk about advertisements for alcohol or cigarettes when you see them. Help children learn to refuse dangerous behaviors and activities.	Teach children their complete name, address, and phone number (including area code). Practice "no, go, yell, tell" by role playing different situations. Walk through the neighborhood with young people identifying safe places. Take them seriously if they ever report feeling scared or uncomfortable.

Systemic Renewal

Systemic renewal is a continuing process of evaluating goals and objectives related to school policies, practices, and organizational structures as they affect a diverse group of learners. The following tool is included in this chapter:

Dropout Prevention Strategies: Self-Assessment Tool (Performance Indicators), developed by Leon Swartz, Director, Schoolwide Accountability Consultants Ltd.; hswarts@iglou.com.

Dropout Prevention Strategies: Self-Assessment Tool (Performance Indicators)

All Grade Levels

Systemic Renewal
All 15 Strategies

The Kentucky Department of Education has developed a rubric using all of the 15 strategies to measure school performance and potential dropouts.

Early Interventions

Standard 1: Family Engagement

Regardless of class, race, and socioeconomic background, most parents have access to social supports and resources that can facilitate their child's achievement. An unbridgeable gap between school and home does not exist.

Identify the level of improvement needed in the district or school for each performance indicator. Mark an (x) below the description that best reflects the degree of improvement needed.

Family Engagement Performance Indicators

Performance Indicators	Little	Some	Moderate	High	Very High
The district/school reaches out to parents so that all students feel they are a part of the learning community.					
The district/school makes students feel they are a part of a "school family."					
The district/school defines family involvement.					
A plan or procedure exists that outlines how to support families.					
Families are encouraged and given an opportunity to promote their involvement.					
Guidelines for effectiveness in family involvement are established.					
Effective programs and practices are identified and used.					

Standard 2: Early Childhood Education

Effective prevention and intervention can make a difference. Formal early childhood programs (day care, preschool, and nursery) are available in the community and in the schools.

Identify the level of improvement needed in the district or school for each performance indicator. Mark an (x) below the description that best reflects the degree of improvement needed.

Early Childhood Education Performance Indicators

Performance Indicators	*Little*	*Some*	*Moderate*	*High*	*Very High*
In-home strategies available within the community are encouraged and reinforced by the district or school.					
Out-of-home strategies (Early Start, Head Start, private programs) are recommended and supported by the district or school.					
The early grades (Pre-K/K–3) provide responsive curricula, content relevance, mixed-age grouping, small class sizes, and parent involvement.					
Out-of-school programs for early childhood education include parenting classes for teens to help develop an understanding of responsibility and to access links to community resources.					
Comprehensive guides for quality standards (i.e., National Association of Young Children) are available and used by the district or school.					
Early childhood education resources, organizations, and models are available and recommended to families.					

Standard 3: Early Literacy Development

Skills are developed in elementary and middle schools and remain a point of emphasis in secondary schools, particularly for at-risk students.

Identify the level of improvement needed in the district or school for each performance indicator. Mark an (x) below the description that best reflects the degree of improvement needed.

Early Literacy Development Performance Indicators

Performance Indicators	Little	Some	Moderate	High	Very High
Reading and writing skills are emphasized as fundamental to effective learning in almost every subject taught in school.					
Reading and writing have received the thoughtful attention of the educational community.					
Reading and writing programs are chosen from a vast number of resources that include a broad range of possible approaches.					
Individual districts and schools identify their specific needs and find an approach or program that works.					
All other strategies for dropout prevention are linked to, receive support, and build on reading and writing.					

Basic Core Strategies

Standard 4: Mentoring and Tutoring

A commitment exists to provide guidance and support to work with youth who need role models and a positive support system.

Identify the level of improvement needed in the district or school for each performance indicator. Mark an (x) below the description that best reflects the degree of improvement needed.

Mentoring and Tutoring Performance Indicators

Performance Indicators	Little	Some	Moderate	High	Very High
The district/school understands why adolescents need mentors.					
Mentoring consists of structured programs to develop relationships and support.					
The district/school establishes goals and expected benefits of mentoring.					
The district/school defines mentoring as a community development program.					
Key components of successful mentoring programs are identified and implemented.					
A planning guide is used to develop mentoring programs that are specifically designed for students who are at-risk of dropping out school.					
Program coordinators recognize the limitations of mentoring programs and are watchful in their planning and implementation.					
Program evaluation is used to measure program progress and its impact on students.					
Mentoring programs are not regarded as an independent intervention or offered as the only effective strategy for working with students in at-risk situations.					

Standard 5: Service Learning

Service learning is used as a teaching methodology to engage youth in their schools and communities by applying their academic knowledge to solve community problems.

Identify the level of improvement needed in the district or school for each performance indicator. Mark an (x) below the description that best reflects the degree of improvement needed.

Service Learning Performance Indicators

Performance Indicators	Little	Some	Moderate	High	Very High
Service learning is used by educators to provide students with experiences that are a "moving force" for real learning and understanding.					
A framework consisting of preparation, action, reflection, and celebration is carefully followed to assist the novice and advanced practitioner.					
The district/school recognizes the impact of service learning on academics and social skills.					
The district/school recognizes the scope and variety of possibilities of service learning and selects effective programs and practices.					

Standard 6: Alternative Schooling

Educational opportunities for at-risk youth "inside the system" are valued and serve students with unique learning interests or disabilities, teenage parents, potential dropouts, violent individuals, or those in juvenile detention systems.

Identify the level of improvement needed in the district or school for each performance indicator. Mark an (x) below the description that best reflects the degree of improvement needed.

Alternative Schooling Performance Indicators

Performance Indicators	Little	Some	Moderate	High	Very High
State legislators, community representatives, the school board, families, and educators are fully committed to alternative schooling.					
These essential questions are considered: (1) What kind of alternative schooling should be offered? (2) What should alternative programs look like? (3) How should they be integrated with the regular school programs?					
State agencies (Department of Juvenile Justice) and community-based programs are identified as a category for alternative schooling.					
Alternative schooling is truly emphasized for its dropout-prevention potential.					
Alternative schooling is available at the elementary, middle, and high school levels.					
A variety of alternative school models are available to serve local needs (i.e., classrooms, school-within-a-school, separate schools, continuation schools).					
Alternative school types are considered during development (educational, disciplinary, therapeutic).					

A consistent profile of educational practices is apparent (i.e., low teacher-to-student ratio, low enrollment, caring staff, flexibility).					
Program evaluations, standards, and impact results are used to measure process and student outcomes.					
Effective program and practices are researched to reinvent learning opportunities and school designs.					

Standard 7: After-School Opportunities

Structured out-of-school experiences and the positive effects of such programs on academic success, social behavior, and opportunities for enrichment of students in at-risk situations are universal practices.

Identify the level of improvement needed in the district or school for each performance indicator. Mark an (x) below the description that best reflects the degree of improvement needed.

After-School Opportunities Performance Indicators

Performance Indicators	*Little*	*Some*	*Moderate*	*High*	*Very High*
Extended day and after-school programs are developed and implemented at elementary, middle, and high school levels.					
Year-round schools, after-school tutoring, mentoring, and community-based programs are available to youth for enrichment opportunities.					
Characteristics of quality out-of-school programs address academic, recreational, and cultural components.					
Implementation considerations such as staff and volunteer training, structure, evaluation, family and child inclusion in planning, and advisory board input are evident.					
Research is conducted to identify effective programs and practices and to explore resources.					

Instruction

Standard 8: Professional Development

Effective and continual high-quality professional development is in place to prepare teachers to help students achieve higher standards.

Identify the level of improvement needed in the district or school for each performance indicator. Mark an (x) below the description that best reflects the degree of improvement needed.

Professional Development Performance Indicators

Performance Indicators	Little	Some	Moderate	High	Very High
A belief and investment in well-qualified teachers in every classroom and at every level exists.					
The definition of high-quality teaching is expressed in the following characteristics: (1) commitment to students and learning, (2) knowledge of the subjects they teach and how to teach them, (3) responsibility for managing and monitoring student learning, (4) systematic thinking about practice and learning from experience, and (5) membership in the learning community.					
Content, quality, and duration are considered rather than fragmentation, limited curriculum focus, and the short term.					
A link between instructional policy and classroom practice exists because professional development is grounded in the curriculum that students study, connected to assessment, and extended in time.					
Components of effective professional development are focused on teachers, leadership, collaboration, and long-term planning and evaluation.					
Research is conducted on effective programs and practices.					

Standard 9: Active Learning

Instruction includes a variety of activities and empowers all students, no matter what there learning style.

Identify the level of improvement need in the district or school for each performance indicator. Mark an (x) below the description that best reflects the degree of improvement needed.

Active Learning Performance Indicators

Performance Indicators	Little	Some	Moderate	High	Very High
The theory of multiple intelligences (Gardner, 1983) is accepted and incorporated into classroom practices.					
The benefits of the theory of multiple intelligences are applied in learning environments to enrich the lives of learners and educational leaders.					
Effective programs and practices are used in a wide variety of settings within and outside the school.					

Standard 10: Educational Technology

Technology is expanded in classrooms in ways that enhance student learning and expand opportunities for all students.

Identify the level of improvement need in the district or school for each performance indicator. Mark an (x) below the description that best reflects the degree of improvement needed.

Educational Technology Performance Indicators

Performance Indicators	Little	Some	Moderate	High	Very High
The "digital divide," that is, the gap between computer accessibility, is bridged by the district or school.					
The potential of technology in the classroom is used to broaden teacher and student access to educational resources.					
Computers are used to supplement instruction, provide differentiated learning, and reach students who otherwise wouldn't like school.					
Technology is used to promote positive attitudes and to promote success for students who may have faced only frustration and failure.					
Technology is used to remove barriers to learning and to enable teachers to customize instruction to a student's individual needs and strengths.					
Various forms of educational technology, such as calculators, word processors, networked multimedia computers, television, and videocassette recorders, are used.					
Inhibitors and resistance to technology exist (cost, professional development, infrastructure, curriculum alignment), but they are not a barrier to use.					
Effective programs and practices are researched and considered.					

Standard 11: Individualized Instruction

Individualized learning has been recognized as an effective educational strategy for all students, especially those who are at risk of dropping out of school.

Identify the level of improvement need in the district or school for each performance indicator. Mark an (x) below the description that best reflects the degree of improvement needed.

Individualized Instruction Performance Indicators

Performance Indicators	Little	Some	Moderate	High	Very High
The district/school practices a belief that all students can learn—if the conditions of learning are such that the individual needs of students (economic and social backgrounds, learning styles, intellectual strengths) are met.					
Individualized Education Plans for special education students are used as a guide to support and services for students with disabilities.					
Consideration is given to the possibility of using Individualized Education Plans with students in at- risk situations.					
Strategies for individualizing students' learning experience, such as mentoring and tutoring, academic interventions, counseling and social services, varying instructional strategies, alternative schools, and instructional technologies, are used in the classroom.					
Explicit provisions or adapting the curriculum to student's particular abilities and needs (such as content emphasis, skill mastery, pacing, learning method, authentic assessment, cooperative learning, and peer tutoring) exists for students who are at risk of dropping out.					

Community Involvement

Standard 12: Systemic Renewal

A coordinated effort is used to harness the forces that can bring about improvement in schools. The essential components of true systemic renewal are identified and examples show how stakeholders can collaborate effectively to ensure that all students can achieve success in school.

Identify the level of improvement need in the district or school for each performance indicator. Mark an (x) below the description that best reflects the degree of improvement needed.

Systemic Renewal Performance Indicators

Performance Indicators	Little	Some	Moderate	High	Very High
Standard-based and whole-school reforms are embraced in the form of high academic expectations for all students, rigorous and challenging tests, and accountability systems that provide incentives and rewards for all stakeholders.					
The district/school recognizes that the critical variables related to improvement, change, and effectiveness are organizational and systemic rather than individual or programmatic in nature.					
Effective programs and practices are researched and used.					
Implementation of systemic renewal requires finding ways (congruence, core of the school, leadership, data driven, community involvement) to create a collaborative mode of work to replace existing isolation and powerlessness under the traditional system.					

Standard 13: School–Community Collaboration

School–community collaboration focuses on the values and pitfalls of collaborative efforts to bring about change and a discussion about the key components of effective community collaboration take place.

Identify the level of improvement need in the district or school for each performance indicator. Mark an (x) below the description that best reflects the degree of improvement needed.

School–Community Collaboration Performance Indicators

Performance Indicators	Little	Some	Moderate	High	Very High
The business of educating children includes the close involvement of parents, businesses, community leaders, politicians, and other special-interest organizations.					
These groups have a shared vision with clearly defined roles, pooling of resources, and a concentration on solutions of selected issues, and they do not generate barriers to reaching that end.					
School leaders actively recruit community collaboration to help study and provide solutions to a multitude of issues ranging from academic achievement to good nutrition for children.					
School and community leaders carefully guide each of the collaborative efforts to be sure it is directed to the same vision of the community, avoiding duplication or wasteful efforts.					
Collaboration is explicitly defined and directed at overall school renewal and targeted issues, such as the high school graduation rate.					
Guidelines for collaboration include ideas about getting started, leadership, staffing, funding, and services.					
Basic components of collaboration are followed, such as shared vision, skilled leadership, process orientation, cultural diversity, membership-driven agenda, multiple sectors, and accountability.					
Educational and community leaders who design and develop community collaboratives look at other model programs and practices.					

Standard 14: Career and Technical Education

Career and technical education is an appropriate blend of solid education competencies and career-based competencies to prepare students for the workforce.

Identify the level of improvement need in the district or school for each performance indicator. Mark an (x) below the description that best reflects the degree of improvement needed.

Career and Technical Education Performance Indicators

Performance Indicators	Little	Some	Moderate	High	Very High
Students are given the opportunity, guidance, and assistance needed to learn the principles of successful job retention.					
The district/school is involved in a major rethinking of the design and delivery of career-oriented education and career-guidance programs.					
A major transition exists in a shift from vocational education to school-to-work programs (tech prep, career academies, apprenticeships, and internships).					
Academic and career-based skills are integrated to raise academic standards for all students.					
Promising measures exist, such as more coherence and focus in the curriculum, encouraging more student-driven projects, opportunities for teacher collaboration, offering a range of curriculum options, and supporting learning opportunities and experiences outside the classroom.					
School-to-work opportunities are available for student transition from school to the work world.					

Standard 15: Safe Learning Environments

Issues of violence and conflict, viewed as factors that contribute to the school dropout problem, are dealt with through a comprehensive program for conflict resolution and violence prevention.

Identify the level of improvement need in the district or school for each performance indicator. Mark an (x) below the description that best reflects the degree of improvement needed.

Safe Learning Environments Performance Indicators

Performance Indicators	Little	Some	Moderate	High	Very High
A high degree of attention is given to making the school a safe place where students can achieve.					
Inappropriate curricular placement, irrelevant academic instruction, or in consistent classroom management within a climate fraught with rigid behavioral demands and insensitivity to student diversity do not exist.					
Conflicts between home and school culture, an ineffective discipline system, negative school climate, retention and suspension, attendance or truancy, behavior and discipline problems, pregnancy, drug abuse, poor peer relationships, high incidence of criminal activity, dysfunctional home lives, and child abuse or ineffective parenting are resolved or managed so that at-risk students will not drop out of school.					
All schools at all grade levels teach violence prevention and conflict resolution to deescalate, manage, and resolve conflicts with adults and peers.					

A comprehensive program for violence prevention and conflict resolution involves key elements such as cooperative thinking, support from agencies, active engagement of all stakeholders, a resource officer, a no-bullying program, a conflict-resolution curriculum, anger-management techniques, peer mediation, elimination or control of gangs, and a crisis-management team.					

List of Contributors

I am deeply indebted to the individuals and organizations whose names appear below. This book could not have been completed had it not been for their contributions. Contact them for further information.

Joselle Alexander, Assistant Director, Children and Youth Initiatives, National Crime Prevention Council, 1000 Connecticut Avenue NW, 13th Floor, Washington, DC 20036, www.ncpc.org.

Center for Mental Health in Schools, Box 951563, Los Angeles, CA 90095-1563. The center is codirected by Howard Adelman and Linda Taylor and operates under the auspices of the School Mental Health Project in the Department of Psychology, University of California, Los Angeles.

Corporation for National and Community Service, Students in Service to America, Washington, DC, www.usafreedomcorps.gov.

Cindy Jones, Education Support Associates, Inc., Des Moines, IA 50309-3382, 515-242-4246, www.educationsupportassociates.com, cindypurcelljones@ earthlink.net.

Angela King, Executive Director, Cannon County REACH Program, 612 Lehman Street, Woodbury, TN 37190, 615-563-5518.

Tom Krubs, Chair, Kansas Learning First Alliance, 1420 SW Arrowhead Road, Topeka, KS 66604, www.teachkansas.org.

Walter McKenzie, Consultant, Surfaquarium, 18 Olde Taverne Lane, Amesbury, MA 01913, www.surfaquarium.com.

National Center for Educational Statistics, *Technology in Schools: Suggestions, Tools and Guidelines for Assessing Technology in Elementary and Secondary Education* (NCES 2003-313), prepared by Tom Ogle, Morgan Branch, Bethann Canada, Oren Christmas, John Clement, Judith Fillion, Ed Goddard, N. Blair Loudat, Tom Purwin, Andy Rogers, Carl Schmitt, and Mike Vinson of the Technology in Schools Task Force, National Forum on Education Statistics, Washington, DC, 2002.

National Council of Research in Vocational Education, University of California, Berkeley, Office of Student Services, and Dennis Dilton, Rock Island High School.

National Education Goals Panel, "Ready Schools," 1255 22nd Street NW, Suite 502, Washington, DC 20037, 202-724-0015, www.negp.gov.

Arnold H. Packer, *School-To-Work* coauthored with Marion W. Pines, M. Frank Stluka, and Christine Surowiec, Eye on Education, 1996.

J. A. Pauley, D. F. Bradley, and J. F. Pauley, *Here's How to Reach Me: Matching Instruction to Personality Types in Your Classroom*, Paul H. Brookes, 2002. Judith Ann Pauley, PhD, Adjunct Professor, California State University, San Marcos, and Joseph F. Pauley, Adjunct Professor, McDaniel College, Maryland.

Joan M. Reid, CFLE, Extension Agent, Family and Consumer Sciences, North Carolina State University, North Carolina Cooperative Extension, Granville County Center, P.O. Box 926, 208 Wall Street, Oxford, NC 27565, 919-603-1350, joan_reid@ncsu.edu.

Rana Sampson, "Bullying in Schools," U.S. Department of Justice, Community Oriented Police Services (COPS), www.cops.usdoj.gov.

David A. Shepard, "Building Parental Support: 50 Ways to Strengthen Your Foundation," The Middle Matters, P.O. Box 22794, Lexington, KY 40522, 859-293-6599.

Dr. Marie Sobers, Transition Coordinator, Alternative Education (703-365-2955), and Dr. Renee Lacey, Supervisor, Alternative Education and Summer School (703-791-8707), Prince William County Schools, Manassas, VA.

Leon Swartz, Director, Schoolwide Accountability Consultants Ltd., hswarts @iglou.com.

Fran Weinbaum, Coordinator, Vermont Consortium for Successful High School Completion.

J. Eileene Welker, MS, CFCS, Assistant Professor, Ohio State University, Tuscarawas County Extension, 419 16th Street SW, New Philadelphia, OH 44663-6403, 330-339-2337, welker.2@osu.edu.

Jennifer Yahn, New Mexico Department of Education, *Working Together: Parent, Family and Community Involvement in Education Tool Kit*, New Mexico Department of Education and the Center for the Education and Study of Diverse Populations, September 2000, Based On the Northern New Mexico Parent Survey, 1996, designed by Eric Romero, NMHU, Las Vegas, NM.

Claus von Zastrow, Senior Program Director, Learning First Alliance, 1001 Connecticut Avenue, Suite 335, Washington, DC 20016, 202-296-5220.

Sally J. Zepeda, *The Principal as Instructional Leader*, Eye on Education, 2003.

Index
By Strategy

Active Learning

Alternative Schooling

After-School Opportunities

Career and Technical Education

Early Childhood Education

Early Literacy Development

Educational Technology

Family Engagement

Individual Instruction

Mentoring-Tutoring

Professional Development

Safe Learning Environments

School-Community Collaboration

Service Learning

Systemic Renewal

Index
By Grade Level

All Grade Levels

Preschool

Elementary School

Middle School

High School

Index
For Administrators

Index
For Counselors

Index For Special Educators